Citizenship and Higher Education

What are the obligations of the university to society and its communities?

What are the virtues of university education?

What are the university's ethical responsibilities to its students?

Citizenship and civic responsibility in higher education are highly contested yet crucial to any consideration of the responsibilities of university education to society at large.

This book offers thoughtful insights into the role of higher education, outlining the intellectual and practical tensions and pressures which come to bear upon higher education institutions. Wide ranging in scope, it offers perspectives from British, European, Canadian and North American contexts.

Citizenship and Higher Education will prove stimulating reading for anyone concerned with the ethics of education and the university's place in society – including educationalists, researchers, sociologists and policy-makers.

James Arthur is Professor of Education and Director of Research at Canterbury Christ Church University College, UK. He is Director of the national citizenship project in teacher education and is author of numerous books on citizenship and ethics.

Karen E. Bohlin is Senior Scholar at Boston University's Center for the Advancement of Ethics and Character, where she is also Adjunct Professor of Education.

Key Issues in Higher Education series
Series editors: Gill Nicholls and Ron Barnett

Books published in this series include:

Citizenship and Higher Education
Edited by James Arthur with Karen E. Bohlin

Defending Higher Education
The crisis of confidence in the academy
Dennis Hayes

Universities and the Good Society
Jon Nixon

The Challenge to Scholarship
Rethinking learning, teaching and research
Gill Nicholls

Citizenship and Higher Education

The Role of Universities in Communities and Society

Edited by

James Arthur

with Karen E. Bohlin

RoutledgeFalmer
Taylor & Francis Group

LONDON AND NEW YORK

First published 2005
by RoutledgeFalmer
2 Park Square, Milton Park, Abingdon, Oxon OX14 4RN

Simultaneously published in the USA and Canada
by RoutledgeFalmer
270 Madison Avenue, New York, NY 10016

RoutledgeFalmer is an imprint of the Taylor & Francis Group

Typeset in Palatino by
Integra Software Services Pvt. Ltd, Pondicherry, India
Printed and bound in Great Britain by
TJ International Ltd, Padstow, Cornwall

British Library Cataloguing in Publication Data
A catalogue record for this book is available from the British Library

Library of Congress Cataloging in Publication Data
A catalog record for this book has been requested

ISBN 0–415–33487–X

Contents

Notes on contributors

John Annette is Professor of Citizenship and Dean of Continuing Education at Birbeck College, University of London. He is researching and publishing currently in the areas of citizenship education in schools and on lifelong learning, service learning and community partnerships in higher education, and on community leadership and involvement in community development and local governance. His latest publication is *Citizenship Education*, co-edited with Sir Bernard Crick and published by Ashgate in 2003. He is the Chair of the CSV's Council for Citizenship and Learning in the Community (CCLC), which is the UK national network of university service learning programmes. He is working internationally for the British Council to promote service learning in higher education in several countries. He is an advisor to the Department for Education and Skills on citizenship education and also to the Active Community Unit of the Home Office on citizenship and community development.

James Arthur is Professor of Education and Director of Research at Canterbury Christ Church University College. He is the director of the national citizenship project in teacher education. He has written on the relationship between theory and practice in education, particularly the links between communitarianism, social virtues, citizenship and education. He is also a member of a number of government advisory committees on citizenship education. His publications include: *Education with Character: The Moral Economy of Schooling* (Routledge), *Schools and Community: The Communitarian Agenda in Education* (Falmer Press), *Social Literacy, Citizenship, and the National Curriculum* (Routledge), *Teaching Citizenship Education through Secondary History* (Routledge), *The Thomist Tradition in Education, Teaching*

Citizenship in the Secondary School, and many articles and chapters in books. He was previously a member of the National Forum for Values in the Community and Education and is a member of the editorial board of the British Journal of Educational Studies.

Karen E. Bohlin is Head of School at Montrose School in Natick, MA, one of the few secondary schools in the United States to earn the distinction of National School of Character in 1999. She served as Director of Boston University's Center for the Advancement of Ethics and Character for several years and is currently a senior scholar at the Center and an adjunct professor of education at Boston University. A former secondary English teacher, Bohlin's most recent book is *Teaching Character Education Through Literature: Awakening the Moral Imagination* (London: RoutledgeFalmer 2004). She is co-author with Kevin Ryan of the widely acclaimed book *Building Character in Schools* (1999) and its companion *Resource Guide* (2001). She has also published articles and research in the *Journal of the Association of Teacher Education, Education Week, The Character Education Partnership, The Journal of Education* and elsewhere. An educational advisor on the national, state and local level, Bohlin has worked closely with schools, educational corporations and state departments of education.

Ian Davies is Senior Lecturer in Educational Studies at University of York, UK. **Peter Cunningham** is Senior Lecturer at London Metropolitan University. **Mark Evans** is Director of Secondary Teacher Education at the University of Toronto. **Gunilla Fredriksson** is International Co-ordinator at Linköping University, Sweden. **Graham Pike** is Dean of Education at the University of Prince Edward Island. **Hanns-Fred Rathenow** (Director of the Institute of Social Sciences and Historical-Political Education) and **Felicitas Tesch** (member of the Berlin Parliament) are based in the Technical University of Berlin. **Alan Sears** and **Pam Whitty** are based in the University of New Brunswick. (An earlier version of Chapter 9 was presented at the conference, 'Lifelong citizenship learning, participating democracy and social change: Local and global perspectives', held at Ontario Institute for Studies in Education (OISE) at the University of Toronto, Canada [17–19 October 2003].)

Charles L. Glenn is Professor of Administration, Training and Policy Studies, and Fellow of the University Professors Program at Boston University. From 1970 to 1991 (including all three Dukakis administrations) he was the director of urban education and equity efforts for the Massachusetts Department of Education, administering over $500 million in state funds for magnet schools and desegregation, and had initial responsibility for the nation's first state bilingual education mandate. Glenn is author of a number of studies in educational history and comparative policy, including *The Myth of the Common School* (1988), *Choice of Schools in Six Nations* (1989), *Educational Freedom in Eastern Europe* (1994, 1995), *Educating Immigrant Children: Schools and Language Minorities in Twelve Nations* (1996) and *The Ambiguous Embrace: Government and Faith-based Schools and Social Agencies* (2000).

Dennis Hayes is the Head of the Centre for Studies in Education and Work at Canterbury Christ Church University College. A philosopher by training, he taught for many years in special schools and in further education. Along with Robin Wynyard he edited a well-received book on *The McDonaldization of Higher Education* and has just completed a book for this series entitled *Defending Higher Education: The Crisis of Confidence in the Academy*. He is part of a team that launched the Pfizer Institute of Idea Debating Matters Competition in 2003–2004 and he has recently led a collaboration of over forty educationalists to produce stimulating and original papers for *The RoutledgeFalmer Guide to Key Debates in Education*.

Terence McLaughlin is Professor of Philosophy of Education in the Institute of Education, University of London. He lectured in philosophy of education for many years at the University of Cambridge and has also taught and held senior positions in two comprehensive schools. He has researched and published widely in philosophy of education and has lectured in over 25 countries and has held visiting positions in universities in the USA, Norway, Spain, Australia and Lithuania. McLaughlin is currently Chair of the Philosophy of Education Society of Great Britain and Convenor of the Steering Group of the International Network of Philosophers of Education.

Arthur Schwartz is Vice President for Research and Programs in the Human Sciences at the John Templeton Foundation. He has been a member of the Foundation's senior staff since 1995 and and previously directed the Foundation's grant award programmes in the area of character development. Previous to joining the Foundation, Schwartz taught at the Harvard Graduate School of Education. He also served for several years as director of dropout prevention programmes for the School District of Philadelphia, and in 1990 Schwartz was recognized for his successful efforts to reduce school dropouts at White House ceremony hosted by President George Bush. Since 1992 Schwartz has concentrated his research on adolescent moral and spiritual development. He has delivered papers at numerous national conferences and published articles in the *Harvard Educational Review, Journal of Moral Education, Educational Record, Liberal Education, Chronicle of Higher Education, Peer Review,* among others. He recently authored the lead chapter in the recently published Hoover Institution volume Bringing in a new era in Character Education.

Martin Thrupp is Senior Lecturer in Education Management and Leadership at the Institute of Education, University of London. His research interests include the nature and impact of educational reform in New Zealand and England, the social and political limitations of educational management literatures and the influence of social class on school processes. He is currently involved in a study of educational autonomy and regulation across five European countries. He is the convenor of the BERA Social Justice SIG and author of *Schools Making a Difference: Let's Be Realistic!* (1999) and, with Rob Wilmott, *Education Management in Managerialist Times: Beyond the Textual Apologists* (2003).

Series editors' preface

The last few years have seen rapid change in both the context and nature of higher education. Characteristically, the debates have been placed in the context of the massification and globalization of higher education, with the debates focusing on such matters as quality assurance, units of resource, access and competence. What have often been lost in such debates have been the aims and values of the university, and the broad purposes of higher education systems and such questions as, what does it mean to be an academic and what it is to learn in a world of change?

It is now timely to refocus on such key issues in higher education for they are universal around the world and perennial in time. This series of books is aimed at addressing these issues, but by placing them in the contemporary context. The series is intended to offer critiques and evaluations of trends in higher education, extending this – wherever possible – to a vision and purpose that higher education could or should be in civic society and a global environment.

The series has been initiated with a set of five books by leading experts in the field of higher education, and *Citizenship and Higher Education* is the first in the series. This book makes a scholarly contribution to the discussion about citizenship in higher education. Each chapter addresses questions of citizenship and civic responsibility together with how universities attempt to shape the lives of their students and society.

Each of the authors believes that the university can and should help students make decisions about their personal lives, about freedom and responsibility and about the kinds of ethical codes that might guide them. They recognize that universities have a wider set of obligations to society, which goes beyond the mere rhetoric of mission statements. A higher education citizenship culture is needed. As Professor Arthur states, 'a "citizenship culture" consists of fundamental democratic and personal values that require students actively to engage in educational experiences that are beyond the realm of measurement'. Considering the level of public investment in higher education in both Britain and the USA, one would expect universities to demonstrate a clear commitment to a culture of citizenship. This book examines the citizenship culture from a number of perspectives in the USA and Britain.

The chapters are written by international scholars and seek to explore the following kinds of questions: What are the wider obligations of the university to society and communities? What are the university's civic and ethical responsibilities? Should the university produce a new generation of leaders who have an interest in promoting the common good? How are universities engaged in service-learning? Should the university be interested in the 'character' of its students? How does the university promote the culture of citizenship? What are the virtues of a university education?

The debates surrounding these questions set challenges to the reader and the higher education community at large. The book will be of interest to all concerned with the place the university holds in a learning and civic society.

Gill Nicholls
Ron Barnett

Chapter 1

Introduction

James Arthur

This collection of essays adds a range of scholarly contributions to the continuing discussion about citizenship in higher education. The essays address questions of higher learning based upon principles of citizenship and civic responsibility together with how universities attempt to shape the lives of their students and society. Consequently, many of the contributors approach the notion of citizenship with a degree of wariness as the term can stand for a range of disparate concepts, none of which are universally accepted. Ahier, Beck and Moore (2003) discuss the problematic nature of theoretical discussions of citizenship and lament the lack of a widely used language of citizenship. It is therefore important that we offer some broad under-standing of citizenship. Citizenship clearly implies membership in a political grouping of some sort, but it is widely recognized that there are tensions between the political-legal language used in describing this membership and the symbolic-affective dimensions of citizenship. Marshall (1950) spoke about 'social citizenship' meaning social and moral identity of the individual situated within a particular community. He emphasized the idea of the 'social self' in citizenship by describing the strong interdependence between the self and society. It is this definition of citizenship that is utilized in many of the chapters in this collection with their emphasis on the moral dimensions of citizenship.

As Hargreaves (1997) observes: 'Active citizens are as political as they are moral; moral sensibility derives in part from political under-standing; political apathy spawns moral apathy.' There is much concern in society that students lack a social consciousness, and that they are driven largely by materialistic values. Some of the contributors in this collection argue that citizenship can offer an alternative path for young people – one that helps them discover who they might or ought to become.

It would seem that the primary responsibility of the university is to educate its students, to expand their knowledge, to teach them to pursue the truth and to develop their intellectual and vocational life. The university can also help students make decisions about their personal lives, about freedom and responsibility and about the kinds of ethical codes that might guide them. In so doing the university actively develops the critical capability of students to think problems through that arise in their lives.

Universities in the USA and UK have long been recognized as having a set of wider obligations to society. They bring huge numbers of young people each year in intimate contact with each other. The provision of academic courses in higher education traditionally has assumed that students will become critical, thoughtful and deliberative citizens able to understand and participate constructively in society. The idea that universities have a civic role has been a feature of their rhetoric, as has been the belief that universities are concerned with more than producing technically skilled graduates. However, the contemporary educational experience of students in higher education suggests that it is not necessary for them to engage with questions of character, civic obligation or conscience. Universities, under increased regulations and financial constraints, are not obliged to incorporate within the students' course anything that is not directly quantifiable. And yet a 'citizenship culture' consists of fundamental democratic and personal values that require students to actively engage in educational experiences that are beyond the realm of measurement.

The increasing technical transformations of higher education raise questions in an acute way about the nature and function of universities in preparing their students for citizenship. There is generally no core curriculum that defines the students' preparation for citizenship and yet the students' participation in teaching and research necessarily involves them at some level in questions particularly relevant to what it is to be a good citizen. What are the fundamental commitments of the modern university? What should universities be expected to teach – that which benefits the individual or those things that benefit society? As Crick (2000a: 145) says, 'Universities are part of society and, in both senses of the word, a critical part which should be playing a major role in the wider objectives of creating a citizenship culture.' It is the view of many of the contributors to this book that universities should help define, build and advance this 'citizenship culture'. It is obvious that not every higher education institution can or should do everything. It is also true that not all education takes place in a classroom or laboratory. As Newman recognized in his *Idea of a University*, the most important educators at any university are peers. Universities often claim that they seek to preserve and enhance a rich social life for their students, but there is more often too rigid a divide between the life of the student residence halls and the life of the classroom and laboratory, between the affective life of student social engagement and the reflective life of the mind.

Aristotle sought the education of free citizens, fully capable of deliberating on the questions of the day, as well as training for occupations so that students could serve the good of the city-state. Aristotle saw education as the means to encourage a commitment by the student to the well-being of the *polis* as well as a willingness to participate in public affairs. Aristotle's definition of citizenship therefore presupposes a society, but it also emphasizes the education of the individual in virtue – the civic virtues of moderation, trustworthiness, judgement, the spirit of protectiveness and goodwill. There is a tension between the Aristotelian virtues and the modern democratic ideal. This latter ideal includes teaching the democratic dispositions of citizenship. Liberal understandings of citizenship today might accept the general aims of a university education, but commit the university to adopt a neutral stance towards competing understandings of the good. However, this 'neutral stance' is generally selective as higher education courses often emphasize the virtues of tolerance, the insistence on inclusion and the appreciation of different cultural and moral perspectives. Discussions of citizenship take place within the context of plurality and diversity and within an intellectual system that lacks criteria for distinguishing truth among competing claims.

Disagreements in universities exist not only about conclusions but also about the principles and methods by which conclusions can be reached.

Considering the level of public investment in higher education in both Britain and the USA, one would expect universities to demonstrate a clear commitment to a culture of citizenship. This would include encouraging students to understand the importance of an active citizenry, but also fully recognizing the centrality of free, rational inquiry in a democracy. However, there are a number of pressures on higher education institutions, which tend to inhibit this commitment. They include the movement from 'university' towards a 'multi-versity', which emphasizes technological expertise and narrow academic specialization, a development that is gradually transforming many first-degree courses into pre-professional training. This in turn binds higher education more tightly to the needs of the economy and the increasing desire of students to be 'educated' for employability. There is also a growing schism between community involvement/service, moral character and expertise – 'savvy or skilfulness' and 'moral character' are treated separately so that scholarship is viewed independently of behaviour as a citizen. In terms of schools, the UK government has adopted a policy of promoting citizenship education and 'education with character'. This will no doubt influence and have implications for developments in higher education. The USA has placed a growing emphasis on character and citizenship education in schools over the past decade, but there is little data that suggest its influence on higher education has been at all significant.

The chapters that follow are written by a number of international scholars and seek to explore the following kinds of questions: What are the wider obligations of the university to society and communities? What are the universities' civic and ethical responsibilities? Should the university produce a new generation of leaders who have an interest in promoting the common good? How are universities engaged in service learning? Should the university be interested in the 'character' of its students? How does the university promote the culture of citizenship? What are the virtues of a university education? Citizenship is primarily about the civil virtues, starting with the relationship between individuals. This is why Ahier, Beck and Moore

(2003: 162) are right when they say, 'To approach citizenship from the perspective of the civil rather than the political is to retrace the primary relationship in the historical development of citizenship and to remind ourselves of its bedrock.'

In Chapter 2, I begin by asking whether British universities can even attempt to promote an idea of 'character' when the rest of society does not. The chapter examines the student experience in university and describes how universities can be a powerful influence in shaping individuals' relationships with each other and their communities. It considers how increasingly university thinking is dominated by an ideology of mass production of skills that could be said to be irreconcilable with character education.

In Chapter 3, Charles L. Glenn develops the concept of character from an American perspective on university education. In particular, he explores the idea that a university should essentially 'stand for something' and that it should encourage both faculty and students to make certain life commitments. He discusses academic freedom and argues that the freedom of a professor to teach is enhanced within a shared framework of meaning.

In Chapter 4, John Annette explores how the British government's social objectives seek to encourage volunteering among students and staff in higher education. Over the next three years British universities will receive funding from The Higher Education Active Community Fund to promote these objectives. Of course, students have long been involved in community work and the national network of Student Community Action has been instrumental in offering volunteering opportunities to students. For the most part, student volunteering has been outside any academic framework, but government policy appears to be aimed at incorporating community action into a more coherent higher education framework. Annette focuses on this interest in community and community involvement within the context of debates about citizenship in higher education.

Arthur Schwartz, Vice President of the Templeton Foundation, has a long experience with service learning programmes in the USA and develops Annette's themes in Chapter 5. The John Templeton Foundation has developed an *Honor Roll* as well as a *Guide to Colleges that Encourage Character Development*. He provides a series of personal insights into the civic values that should guide a university.

John Annette and Terence McLaughlin provide us with a second chapter (Chapter 6) to introduce a discussion of citizenship in British higher education from a communitarian perspective. After exploring ideas of what citizenship might mean, Annette and McLaughlin move to a consideration of civil renewal within higher education and draw on the work of scholars in the USA. Annette and McLaughlin advocate active citizenship that encourages HE students to develop skills of civic and political participation, but ask whether, in fact, they appear in the university curriculum.

Karen E. Bohlin, in Chapter 7, provides another US perspective, but focuses on the classical idea of virtue as the moral and intellectual excellences that allow human beings to flourish. She raises the question as to whether virtue can be taught in the university and what a professor's responsibility is towards his or her students. She explores a number of themes in the student's university experience and considers the influence of student choices and motivations. Bohlin argues that it is legitimate for university professors to be concerned with the kinds of people students are becoming.

In Chapter 8, Dennis Hayes provides a contrasting perspective to Karen E. Bohlin's, but whilst he disagrees with many who are advocating 'virtue ethics', he agrees that many academics have given up their academic authority in favour of accepting the students' perspectives as equal to their own. Hayes believes that higher education has become an 'engagement to teach nothing', and as a result he concludes that many of today's students will know nothing worthy of transmission to the next generation.

The chapter on student exchanges (Chapter 9) by Davies *et al.* provides a concrete example of how students in higher education can broaden their horizons on citizenship through exchange programmes. The exchange programme described in this chapter involves no less than seven higher education institutions collaborating with each other in Canada, Sweden, Germany and England. The chapter provides evidence of how student views of citizenship changed as a result of experiencing a different culture. The final chapter (Chapter 10) by Martin Thrupp provides an interesting commentary and critique of managerialism in British higher education and the compromises made by academics because of it. He suggests that the ethical dilemmas academics face, especially when collaborating closely with government policies, might prevent them acting as 'critics and conscience'. There are important implications for any culture of citizenship in higher education in Thrupp's analysis, especially a university's role in developing community and character and the notion of social citizenship.

Chapter 2

Student character in the British University

James Arthur

The direction in which we have been going in the last two decades, under financial pressures growing more and more serious, and government directives more and more compelling, may produce for us thousands and thousands of graduates able to solve technical problems disinterestedly. But they may well regard larger questions, which cannot be made into technical ones as if they were quite marginal. Such refusal to face the truth could, I suggest, in the long run destroy not merely the university and higher education, but essentially, humankind itself.

Niblett (1990)

Introduction

The purpose of higher education appears more intellectual than moral, especially as universities appear not to be able to draw on any consensus, in an age of moral relativism, to shape the decisions that affect their ethical character. The intellectual aims of a university define the limits of what a university can do. It can teach knowledge about morality, but it does not necessarily teach one to practise the precepts of any particular set of morals. Students are also, at least technically, adults, so on what basis in British society can we teach values to a random group of adults? Nevertheless, whilst universities are indeed not convents or seminaries, they of necessity have an ethos, good or bad, that influences the students in them. It is also expected that universities will have certain duties to society that include moral responsibility for those who frequent them. Indeed, universities hold up various moral criteria by which to define the educational task in which they are engaged – education for freedom, education for citizenship, education for the good life, education for character and so on. The crucial question is: Can universities attempt to define and promote an idea of 'character' when the rest of society does not?

According to Barnett (1990: 191), the liberal conception of higher education, education of the whole person, has both conservative and radical interpretations. The conservative interpretation tends towards defining higher education as character formation, whilst the 'radical conception … amounts to nothing less than a total transformation and emancipation of the individual student'. But it appears to me that this 'transformation' of the student is above all concerned with character formation. Barnett, in fact, believes that no such radical conception exists in British higher education, chiefly, I suspect, because of the unrealistic nature of this kind of radical individualism. It is also doubtful whether character formation is still an explicitly and widely recognized aim in higher education, especially with the 'narrowing of vision of what higher education has to offer' (Barnett, 1990: 105). In addition, the business corporate model that operates within many parts of British higher education may also tend to neglect those purposes of a university education that aim to help develop the character of students.

This should not mean that higher education ought therefore to abandon the quest for a defensible and humane form of character development. Universities can be a powerful influence in shaping individuals' relationships with each other and their communities and they have many opportunities to develop basic human qualities for the benefit of both their students and society. Through the provision of academic courses in higher education, it has often been assumed that students will become thoughtful and critical citizens able to understand and participate constructively in democratic society. This chapter suggests that such an assumption requires critical review. It traces the way British universities have been concerned with the development of student character and reviews the extent to which universities are directly and indirectly involved in promoting the character of their students. It also asks what it would mean for higher education to do something seriously about character development.

Many will still ask whether it is the duty of higher education to help form its students' characters and also for what purpose this effort should be undertaken? It is recognized at the outset that this is both a complex and vast area for debate and discussion. The last twenty years have seen great and rapid social change and consequently any discussion of student character inevitably involves many complex background conditions in society such as changing attitudes to authority, to parents, to religion, etc. There has certainly been a decline in convention and precedent in working practices. High-profile scandals in business, medicine, teaching and many other areas of public life add to the loss of confidence and the erosion of trust in traditional institutions. It is perhaps also why conduct in public life is more rigorously scrutinized in an attempt to enforce standards of acceptable behaviour. Some would argue that the good society or a moral tradition must form an essential backdrop for the development of character in higher education. Therefore, to enter a discussion about character in higher education might seem like entering a minefield of conflicting definitions and hollow ideology.

There is the question of how to define or what is meant by character, and I present an honest statement of my own position. First, that there is such a thing as character, an interlocked set of personal values that normally guide conduct. Character is about who we are and who we become. Second, that this is not a fixed set easily measured or incapable of modification, even whilst in university. Third, those choices about conduct are choices about 'right' or 'wrong' actions and thoughts. I believe that we are inescapably involved in forming the character of ourselves and others whilst in university. Character formation does not imply lack of student consent or full participation. My argument is that character development in the modern British university should not simply be about the acquisition of academic and social skills, for it is ultimately about the kind of person a student becomes. It is to do with humans having a purpose that is beyond being an instrument or tool in social processes. This is not achieved within a vacuum, for as Sanford (1969: 8) observes: 'In order to become a person, an individual needs to grow up in a culture, and the richer the culture the more of a person he has a chance of becoming. The central purpose of institutions of higher education is to educate (adults as well as young people); and the aim of education is to develop each individual as fully as possible, to make man more human.' Reeves (1988: 35, 86) notes that 'education cannot "make a person", it has a more limited role'; she concludes that universities should create an environment where ethical development commands parity of esteem with mental development. Both Sanford and Reeves locate character formation within society as a whole. The responsibility for character development is therefore something higher education shares with society.

Character development is about the kind of person we become in a particular kind of community. It is also about the kind of ethical understandings and commitments that are possible for us within that community. Character implies that we are free to make ethical decisions – it is not merely about controlled behaviour. Whilst character is largely formed in early socialization, the experience of higher education continues to influence what and who the student becomes. In outlining the British tradition of character development in higher education, it is first necessary to take a historical approach.

Character in the British higher education tradition

The character of its students is what the British University has tradition- ally claimed to help shape, but whilst it has been a much-repeated claim, it only made a formal appearance in Oxford and Cambridge during the 1860s. A more heightened concern for the development of character coincided with a number of so-called progressive reforms, including the abolition of the religious tests for entry into these two ancient universities. As they began to emerge as modern univer- sities, abandoning their clerical image, they appeared to take their responsibilities for the academic and moral/personal development of their growing student membership more seriously. Academic staff rediscovered their duties *in loco parentis* for those *in statu pupillari* and each college provided every student with the equivalent of a 'moral tutor' to emphasize that it was indeed a caring community. This was of course much influenced by the reforms in the public schools, particularly the influence of Thomas Arnold in promoting the formation of the Christian 'noble character'. Unfortunately, it often amounted to little more than the self-consciously painful display of the required manners by dons and by students in many cases only to those they considered their elders and betters. The development of one's 'character' in the Victorian age tended to be a class-bound concept; it often concerned itself with forced behaviour that removed the elements of freedom and judgement essential for character (Arthur, 2003).

John Henry Newman had previously, in the late 1820s, developed an older model for tutoring students that placed emphasis on both their academic and moral supervision. Newman sought to develop the 'pastoral' responsibility role of tutors. What he meant by the term 'pastoral' was essentially an extension of the role derived from the vow ministers of the Church of England made at ordination. Of course it was these ministers who exclusively made up the fellows of the colleges. Tutors had traditionally been seen as both lecturers and disciplinary officers. In theory, every tutor in a college was supposed to be responsible for the training, in the fullest sense of the word, of the students entrusted to him by the college Head. In practice, this charge, owing to the indifference of the tutors on the one hand, and the indiscipline of the students on the other, amounted to nothing very much (Bouyer, 1958: 85).

It was certainly difficult in the mid-nineteenth century to influence the conduct of the 'gentlemen-commoners' in Oxford who effectively did as they pleased. Any control over the students was less moral than purely disciplinary, exercised largely through a complex system of fines for offences committed. Newman's attempt to get to know his students and to help develop and form their characters both spiritually and morally, whilst popular with his students, did not find favour with Dr Hawkins, the Provost of Oriel. Newman's experiment was, therefore, short-lived, but was revived in new forms in the 1860s. Arnold and Newman, both fellows of Oriel, could therefore be said to have influenced the development of the idea of the 'moral tutor' in universities. Both believed that there had been a decline in the character of students and that what was needed was the Christian moral regeneration of the individual and society. Newman wrote in *The Office and Work of Universities*: 'An educational system without the personal influence of teachers upon pupils, is an arctic winter; it will create an ice-bound, petrified, cast-iron University and nothing else' (1856: 11).

Newman in his *Discourses on the Scope and Nature of University Education*, first given as a series of lectures in 1851, commented that if he had to choose between two university courses – one non-residential, but intellectually challenging (the new University of London!), and the other residential, but intellectually disorganized (the University of Oxford!) – he would prefer the latter. He explains his choice thus:

> When a multitude of young men, keen, open-hearted, sympathetic, and observant, as young men are, come together and freely mix with each other, they are sure to learn one from another, even if there be no one to teach them; the conversation of all is a series of lectures to each, and they gain for themselves new ideas and views, fresh matter of thought, the distinct principles for judging and acting, day by day ...
>
> (cited in Ker, 1989)

Newman believed this 'youthful community' would represent a 'living teaching' and that subsequent generations of students would have their characters influenced and formed by it.

In these lectures he was of course referring to the Oxbridge collegiate system and to young Christian gentlemen, although Newman disliked the word 'gentlemen'. It was a notion of university defined as an exclusive teaching institution. Rothblatt (1968: 247) accurately sums up the purposes of an Oxbridge education in his commentary on Cambridge: 'Education in Cambridge was both university and collegiate, the former professional in its objectives, the latter concerned with character formation.' Dons were expected to be engaged in both types of teaching. Consequently, it must be questioned whether Newman's idea of a university has much of a modern resonance considering the great diversity that constitutes the student body in universities today. Students are no longer a well-defined group with common backgrounds and many courses are now vocationally orientated. Nevertheless, most universities and colleges since Newman's time have actively sought the expansion of student residences, in part, to provide some form of this 'living teaching' tradition together with assisting students in their more general developmental and personal growth. Wardens and tutors in these halls of residence were once specifically selected for their personal qualities or character (see Brothers, 1971). More recently, there has been a dramatic reduction in institution-owned residences for students.

In the Scottish universities tutors had a broad licence over both the intellectual and the moral dimensions of student character and, as Thomas Read observed, tutors were made responsible for 'the whole Direction of their studies, the Training of the Mind, and the Over-sight of their Manners' (cited in Camic, 1983: 171). However, the universities of St Andrews, Glasgow, Aberdeen and Edinburgh had begun to reform themselves during the early part of the eighteenth century and introduced the Professorial system. The old practice of 'academic disputation' was abolished and professors now delivered a course of lectures on a range of topics. The dependency culture of the old tutorial relationship between tutor and student also gradually disappeared. Importantly, the students themselves established numerous societies for inquiry and discussion. The universities were open to every social class and the development of independence, self-reliance, self-improvement and a commitment to community were all promoted by most of the professors as obligatory for students. This is perhaps one reason why Scottish universities often produced strong characters during this period embodying unambiguous civic respon-sibilities. The Scottish university departed markedly from the English model, seeking to form more egalitarian types with a strong sense of public duty and service. Oxbridge only moved to explicit notions of duty and service to society by means of university and college education in the latter part of the nineteenth century. As Barnett (1990: 105) says, 'The English model looked primarily to the eventual social role of the graduate as a "gentlemen", and the face-to-face interaction between student and tutor was crucial.' It was Benjamin Jowett, Master of Balliol College from 1870, who actively promoted the idea of the character of the publicly spirited liberal gentlemen, largely by emphasizing public duty and playing down the Christian dimensions.

The new universities in England, beginning with University College, London, in the nineteenth century and the provincial universities established in the first two decades of the twentieth century from already flourishing colleges, separated their goals for a university education from any religious principles, particularly those of the established Church. Nevertheless, they were no less concerned with the character of their students. When a new university abandoned religious goals, it would invariably establish a completely new set of standards that become disciplinary rather than moral. The Oxbridge system of moral tutors was adopted enthusiastically by a number of these new universities and there were unwritten rules for behaviour with moral tutors responsible for enforcing them. Students were expected to behave well, dress soberly and work hard and they could expect fines, as in the Oxbridge system, if they did not conform. There was a marked paternalism in these new universities and they attempted to guide student feeling as well as thinking. Lecturers had a duty to accept some responsibility for the development of the student outside of the purely academic. However, as Stephen Bailey (cited in Faust and Feingold, 1969: 147) observes, 'the defects of the British approach to character education are easy to spot in retrospect. They are largely summed up in the word "elitism"'. The nineteenth century conception of higher education, which continued into the twentieth century, was, according to Barnett (1990: 105), a cultural experience for the student who was invited to share a common inheritance and participate in 'developmental enrichment' since the student was understood as 'being actively and personally involved in a process larger than himself, whether in interaction with others or directly with knowledge itself'.

A small proportion of students expected ethical standards to be enforced and complained when their university did not provide experiences for their own personal development. For example, E. M. Williams, student editor of the *Tamesis* (1937: 32, 105–106) at the University of Reading, declared in the editorial of this student magazine:

> Considered in the light of its alarming failure to exert any cultural influence upon the majority of its students, we are not sure that the modern university is a good argument for popular education. A fair proportion of these students come from classes to whom a university education would not have been accessible much before the beginning of the present century. They now come up to acquire a varying veneer of specialised knowledge, which has little

visible influence upon their general mental habits. We are not suggesting for a moment that a university should turn them into snobs who speak as if they had been educated at a bad public school, but need they be so ready to revert to type? Take away one man's Physics, and another's History, and another's English... and you have the original shopkeeper, or bank clerk or bus driver or whatnot, neither better nor worse than the original, and retaining all those cultural and moral limitations which it should have been the business of the university to remove.

The National Union of Students Congress in 1939, largely under the influence of Communist Party control, also agreed that the development of student activities should be planned in such a way as to promote their social responsibilities. The universities themselves were conscious of these duties, and in 1947 the University of Birmingham still spoke of character formation as a goal of a university education (Hinton, 1947: 196). Each of the University Grants Committee Reports for 1948, 1952 and 1964 explicitly mentions character development as an aim of higher education. However, the Robbins Report (1963) believed that personal development was primarily brought about by strengthening intellectual activities. Today it may be that the words 'moral' and 'academic' have a restricted range of meanings among modern university students; often 'moral' simply means 'regulations' to them, with the term 'academic' often understood as skills as opposed to the pursuit of truth.

The polytechnics of the late 1960s and 1970s were partly established in response to the needs of industry and had a more explicit economic service function as opposed to a focus on wider social and cultural functions; An emphasis on vocationalism, as opposed to a liberal education. They provided students with the skills and qualifications required by an industrialized economy. Their student bodies often had limited accommodation and facilities, and character development was not an explicit concern they had. Nevertheless, many did emphasize the beneficial effects on character of work well done by promoting the gospel of work. Decency and sobriety were important virtues that they promoted. As the polytechnics became universities in the 1990s, many of them expanded their limited student services whilst continuing to offer professional training courses in which the lecturers explicitly or otherwise concerned themselves with the basic values of the profession they taught their students. These values were not generally framed in terms of ethical values, but were rather instructions in the mores and customary expectations of their trades.

Character and higher education in the twenty-first century

Universities and colleges are today large, open and diverse institutions. These institutions are subject to unprecedented centralized planning, internal bureaucratic administration, and as a consequence largely justify themselves and are judged in the practical areas that can be measured. It is hard to be sure whether the wider community, the student or the university bureaucracy benefits the more from investment in higher education. The great diversification of courses now offered by universities has resulted in the transmission of what can be learnt by students in fragmented fields of study and students are viewed by many as customers. Often the student is left as a consumer investing their time and money in higher education in order to receive some future economic benefit. Abbs (1997) believes that a new managerial elite runs universities with little interest in pursuing the moral purposes of higher education. The emphasis is increasingly seen to be on learning the habits of thinking within a particular discipline, not on the formation of the person. There has been a narrowing of university education to the quantifiable, with teaching often limited to cognitive information or academic skills. In fact, the ideal of learning has, for many, crowded out the ideal of personal development. This is perhaps not surprising, as universities and colleges do not generally present a normative view of the person that could be desired as the goal of higher education and therefore have few stated moral commitments. Modern university education appears to be gravitating to the factory ideal as opposed to the academy. A lecture-based university is essentially about something being done to the student (hence the economic parallel with the service industry) rather than something being done with the student (in a tutorial/ seminar the tutor leads and learns too). The loss of collegial life has also seriously limited the influence of the modern university on character development.

The community that makes up a modern university has also changed dramatically in recent years and perhaps reflects a new kind of society. Perry (1989) asks whether the development of character is more dependent on the characteristics of the students who enter the university rather than the influence of the university itself. The student body in a university is often, as Barnett (1974: 198) says, 'an instructional and chance interaction' community for the purposes of learning. There also appears to be a 'student culture' that permeates all higher education institutions that results in greater resistance to any attempts at overtly influencing the students personally. Academic staff have less direct contact with the ever-increasing number of students and the very idea, provision and use of moral or personal tutors have largely been questioned or even abandoned entirely in some universities. As morality is seen as a private matter, many tutors are less interested in the unquantifiable labours of forming or developing students. In any case, universities themselves are often so large that lecturers are in a weak position to influence their students' values. The affective virtues are consequently rejected by many academics as irrelevant to their task and few books published on higher education talk about ethics in relation to students.

A brief survey of the 2002 mission statements of some British universities indicates that they generally claim to serve the needs, including social needs, of the regions in which they are situated. Many also directly address the question of personal development goals for their student community. Royal Holloway College aims to provide 'an environment which nurtures...the personal development of its students...', whilst Manchester University seeks 'the development of the personal...skills of our students' in addition to 'the fulfilment of civic and regional responsibilities'. Bournemouth University aims to 'develop the full potential of its students' whilst Birmingham University promotes their 'social and cultural well-being' with a 'commitment to truth, wisdom and academic freedom'. Middlesex University boldly calls itself a 'student-centred university' and many other universities and colleges are eager to promote themselves as caring communities providing their students with facilities so that they can serve the local community through active participation in voluntary activities such as Student Community Action and Students into Schools. Research would indicate that moral reasoning is one kind of thinking that appears to be enhanced – *qualitatively* – by this service learning.

The opening words of the Dearing Report (National Committee of Inquiry into Higher Education, 1997) recognized the ethical dimension of higher education by explicitly referring to the purposes of higher education as 'life-enhancing', contributing to the 'whole quality of life' so that students can 'achieve personal fulfilment'. Dearing placed two purposes of higher education alongside each other: the development of intellectual capabilities and at the same time equipping students for work in ways that would help to shape democratic, civilized and inclusive society. Dearing saw higher education institutions as part of the conscience of a democratic society, founded on respect for the rights of the individual and the responsibilities of the individual to society as a whole. It was therefore unfortunate that he then proceeded to ignore most of these moral dimensions by focusing almost exclusively on the instrumental purposes of higher education in the report. Nevertheless, Dearing appears to have implicitly recognized the major change from 'virtuous character' to 'personal fulfilment', and from 'common good' to 'private good'; a recognition that there is no longer a perceived shared sense of the common good and that there is a resistance to any value system that might supersede individual interests.

Universities would still claim that they are promoting the common good and that they retain a civic role that serves the community. They claim that they are preparing students for an active role in a diverse democracy and that they are concerned to produce students who have ethical standards, a sense of social responsibility and well-developed civic competences, who can communicate effectively with others who are different from themselves. Universities might still even claim to help shape students' lives and through them inevitably society. Barnett (1990: 8–9) included 'the student's character formation' among the ten background values traditionally associated with higher education. He draws attention to one of the main functions of higher education, which is the development of the individual. If universities are to achieve these goals, then they need to incorporate experiences into the education of their students that enhance the 'virtue' that forms their 'characters' in the 'service' of the 'common good'. However, these words sound archaic and anachronistic in the modern university even if they were the primary reason why universities found public support for their establishment.

There is much to be learnt from American approaches to character development in higher education. The John Templeton Foundation Initiative on College and Character, for example, seeks to inspire students to live ethical and civic-minded lives. The Character Clearinghouse in the United States also provides character development resources and programmes for higher education institutions. There is still a view that British universities exist to develop human qualities in people as well as for advancing knowledge that enables them to make a contribution to society. The challenge they face is to design a process of character development to fit the complexity of university life today. There could be said to be four levels or issues that together influence the kind of student character development provided in universities and colleges. They are institutional mission, subject/professional studies, student experience and transition from school to university.

Institutional mission

The idea of a university providing formal lectures on character or ethical development might be seen, as Warnock (1975: 435) says, 'as something presumptuous'. She rejects the idea of moral education as a formal part of university life, but nevertheless feels that it should be 'hoped and practised' in a university. Students should be imbued with the ethical ethos of a university, making any formal and compulsory ethics course in the academic curriculum unwarranted. In any case McIntyre (1982) says that universities fail to provide a 'compelling argument' for moral commitments of any kind as notions of morality are contested. Nevertheless, universities still have to address questions of students cheating, altering figures in experiments and copying, not to mention other more serious infringements. Through regulations on these issues the university could be said to be promoting character in its students, but this is merely a disciplinary mode as opposed to a positive attempt to develop the virtues of character. Universities are not neutral places and there is growing pressure on them to contribute to the 'needs of society', but when society's values have collapsed what is meant by the 'needs of society' become uncertain. Higher education has indeed a set of values and a 'hidden curriculum' that conveys moral messages to students and influences their character. Colby (2002) addresses some of the objections often raised to higher education's involvement in promoting core ethical values and demonstrates that students are subjected to a process of socialization that influences their character. Universities, through their mission statements, structure and cultural life exercise an influence on their students' character formation.

It is one reason why the Higher Education Foundation has focused on the ethical purposes of higher education and has called on universities to develop the moral abilities of students. In evidence to the National Committee of Inquiry into Higher Education (The Dearing Report), the Foundation (1997) essentially endorsed the view that 'education is basically a moral relationship between persons devoted to truth'. That is, higher education should produce individuals with 'personal integrity' who understand the consequences of their actions as human beings. The Foundation is concerned with the capacity of higher education to educate the whole person so that they become or develop as responsive people serving the public. The Higher Education Foundation (1997: 11) outlined four sets of abilities that it believed underpinned higher education: intellectual, moral, aesthetic and practical. Under the moral abilities the following list was provided:

The ability to make ethical judgements and accept responsibility;
The exercise of freedom, of personal autonomy, achieving personal fulfilment;
The building of self and community awareness, self-responsibility;
The formation of trust and teamwork.

These abilities were in turn linked to serving the community and are exactly the kinds of abilities that the Scottish universities in the eighteenth century sought to develop in their students. Scholarship was also defined as an ethic of openness, respect for others, a concern for the common good, and personal responsibility for the use of research findings. Unfortunately, there is a modern schism in the university between scholarship and moral character as scholarship is increasingly viewed independently of behaviour as a citizen. It could be argued that this largely individualistic, technical and morally disinterested understanding of the purposes of higher education serves to reinforce this schism as does the control and manufacture of 'research' outputs by corporate funders.

The professionalization of student welfare, counselling, medical and advisory services in universities together with more traditional chaplaincies has also resulted in academics having even less concern for and ability to influence the personal growth and development of their students. The provision of campus facilities that assist students in their more general developmental growth may indicate to the student that the university cares about them, but these are 'services' they may or may not need and they certainly cannot replace positive human contacts within a community. Indeed, proliferation of pay-by-use services in universities leads one to ask what are the business ethics of universities themselves? The provision of personal tutor arrangements provides students with human contact that is not intended to be about therapeutic skills or psychological expertise. Communication of values that help develop the students' character takes place largely through the example of tutors. However, some have argued that recent changes in higher education have resulted in a culture that systematically devalues personal tutor relationships on the basis that students should be responsible for their own development and choices and that academic staff should be free to pursue their research interests (see Cotterill and Waterhouse, 1996: 228). There is also the student code of practice or regulations of a university that can help reinforce any ethos that the university consciously wishes to promote. Nevertheless, it is doubtful whether regulations alone have the power to promote moral sensitivity and ethics in students. The mission statement of a university that includes both intellectual enquiry and personal development goals requires more than the production of disciplinary regulations that simply define areas of permissible conduct.

Subject/professional studies

Whilst disciplinary studies in universities are primarily focused on cultivating a particular branch of learning in the student, they can also directly influence student personal development. Academic disciplines act to socialize students to the prevailing norms and values of the respective academic environment that they have chosen. Eljamal *et al.* (1999) in their study of goals for students' intellectual development in higher education found that academic departments set goals relating the discipline to the student's personal life. They also found that goals were also set to broaden the students' horizons and that these were connected with personal development areas such as increasing student motivation, self-confidence and clarifying values. The humanities-based subjects appeared to be most effective in helping students to 'grow personally'. It may be the case that if physics, or any other scientific discipline, is taught as a field of purely factual knowledge, independent of social, cultural and political contexts, the ethical bearings of the knowledge may be lost for the student. All subjects ought to have a philosophy (of law, biology, etc.) as it is the only way learners will come to understand the enterprise they are engaged in, as opposed to just being technicians, and it is what keeps learning intellectually joined up with the human enterprise. The loss of philosophy or reflection is the victory of the technician qualification over the university degree.

Nevertheless, the requirement to teach ethics is a growing one throughout the higher education sector. Pressure on academic departments to provide for the teaching of ethics comes from a number of sources, including a number of subject benchmarking statements together with professional associations placing a requirement for the inclusion of ethics in the training curriculum of universities. The medicine benchmark states that: 'graduates need to apply ethical and legal knowledge to their practice, particularly in: applying principles of confidentiality, consent, honesty and integrity...'. This list of virtues is written partly to influence the character of the kinds of people who study medicine. However, discussions of ethics within medical courses can be reduced to the themes of rules, of prescriptions and prohibitions for coping with patients, keeping records, avoiding malpractice claims and other similar issues.

The personal style of tutors in academic departments also continues to have an influence on a student's personal development and consequently on forming their characters. Universities do not develop student academic skills in a vacuum for the intellect or mind is rooted in the whole person – a person in community and culture. Consequently, speculative enquiry in a particular subject becomes narrowly focused when it neglects to aim at those goals necessary for the discharge of one's personal and social duties. To simply design a university curriculum or course on purely technical and instrumental requirements serves only to limit student experiences and therefore their personal development. Analytical and disinterested scientific or scholarly expertise will not therefore produce the character of a good citizen. However, it has to be recognized that many students are interested in being educated or trained for employability and many first-degree courses are therefore being transformed into pre-professional training schemes.

These courses for the various professions invariably attempt to address ethical development issues. For example, the Teaching Standards issued by the Department for Education and Skills (2002) for training newly qualified teachers indicate that newly qualified teachers must demonstrate that they can 'treat pupils with respect and consideration'. Standard 1.3 states that teachers must 'demonstrate and promote positive values, attitudes and behaviour that they expect from pupils'. In other words, they must act as adult role models in and beyond the classroom. Whilst there is no explicit reference to the development of character, it is clear that this is what is intended by this standard. There is an implicit recognition in these teaching standards that the character of the teacher matters and that pupils will acquire the habits of good character directly from teachers who embody the ideals of character to which they expect their pupils to aspire. How do higher education institutions respond to these particular standards, especially when the suggestion is that students can be taught professional ethics without at the same time being required to study moral reasoning? The standards are, if you like, an attempt to coerce students into operating within a set of professional codes of conduct, with no requirement that they understand what might underpin such codes. Nor can we conclude that ethical practice is now the highest priority in teacher training courses. What personal values does higher education promote in professional courses in medicine, law, health, business studies, etc.? In the universities, medical and law degrees were not professional courses, but a science and a liberal art. Professional courses began in non-university settings. University education was a preliminary to professional qualification, but not backwashed by it. Much of the discourse in these professions has been conducted in recent years in terms of 'competences', 'skills' and 'outcomes', with little attention paid to purpose and to questions of meaning. The focus is often on what the trainee can do, rather than what the trainee is and can become.

It is often assumed that a profession is inextricably bound up with widely shared values, understandings and attitudes, and therefore to claim the standing of a professional must mean adherence to an ethic, a moral principle, which derives from freely undertaken commitments to serve others as individual human beings, worthy of respect, care and attention. It is also often stated that professions are located within a set of beliefs, values, habits, traditions and ways of thinking that are shared and understood by those already in the profession, but which are seldom articulated. That what we do as professionals will shape who we are as persons and consequently our character does not remain unaffected by our professional role actions. Moreover, when a code of professional ethics becomes autonomous from our personal moral norms, rather than being a particular application of them, then we are left with an institutional morality that can lead to mechanical role morality, rather along the lines described by Niblett (1990: 20) with 'thousands and thousands of graduates able to solve technical problems disinterestedly'. Some would even suggest that professional ethics is a collective attempt to contextualize ordinary morality into the particular professional outlook – it is about applying personal ethics to the context of the professional role. This last statement conflicts with the idea that doctors should follow the advice of their Medical Defence Association, which is to drive past traffic accidents.

These arguments about the ethical meaning of professionalism on closer scrutiny are perhaps far too optimistic and are simply repeating a myth. The history of the English professions shows that a code of conduct was part of their incorporation in the nineteenth century, of essentially artisan trades who adopted the corporate ethical community structure of the medieval corporation. But the codes of conduct were never the sedimenting of a popular morality, rather the selection of a heraldic badge for display and flaunting. When has the English solicitor, in literature, ever been seen as anything other than carrion?

The kinds of virtues they adopted were generally of the narrowest kind and concerned almost totally with public probity. Today, when a profession has a code it often excuses its members to think about the ethical issues involved. And yet professional codes speak of obligations or parties to whom obligations are owed. The difficulty is that since the terms used in these codes lack practical definitions the strength of these obligations are also unclear.

Nevertheless, professional actions can be a choice of whom to become as a person. Indeed, the decision about who to be precedes the decision about what to do, for our moral character is the foundation of ethical actions. Can a university course that prepares students for teaching, medicine, law, business and much else besides address these questions? In the contemporary culture of Britain can higher education have a role infusing the discourse of commerce and politics with a moral dimension, through the development of the character of its students? Whether it is academic study or professional preparation, moral issues are integral to the material studied and it is clear that student sensitivity is being shaped through them, but whilst they may be encouraged to be intellectually alive to moral issues, this is not the same as developing an ethical character. It is often said that the moral dimension of being a professional entails a dedication to a particular way of life, a commitment to better one's profession, and a willingness to put the needs of society before the interests of oneself. Since universities have a major role in the preparation and continuing education of the workforce, it is essential that they address these moral issues.

Student experience

What are the motivations of students and staff for study at university? In the *Confessions*, St Augustine concerns himself with the intentions which ought and ought not to guide the student in his or her pursuit of knowledge. One reason offered is the pursuit of knowledge to impress classmates and academic staff – in other words the vice of pride. Another is the encouragement of parents and academics who want education for their children in order for them to achieve worldly success. The second reason would appear to be the more prevalent one today. In an early study of 205 students at Oxford and Manchester universities in 1963, Zweig (1963: XIIIff) found that students were conscientious and aware of their moral and social responsibilities. He reported that students were honest, sincere, self-disciplined and had an 'altruistic frame of mind'; that they were searching for a 'service to render', in short, that 'They feel they ought to repay society by being good scientists or good civil servants, teachers or industrialists, and contributing to higher standards of culture.' Zweig (1963: 190) concludes that the ethos of the 'model student' in a university should be, among other things, co-operative, self-confident, emotionally stable and altruistically minded. However, he says very little about what role universities have in developing these qualities.

As the sixties progressed, not all shared Zweig's rather idealistic view of student character. Malcolm Muggeridge, in the course of his final rectorial address in the University of Edinburgh, denounced the students for their sloth and self-indulgence. He found their 'demand for pot and pills ... the most tenth-rate sort of escapism and self-indulgence ever known' (cited in Ingrams, 1995: 207). In a more contemporary study Henry (1994: 110–111) examined the student experience in higher education from an ethical perspective and found that students understood that there are moral implications for them as part of higher education, particularly in the realm of respect for persons, and that most students felt that all should be valued irrespective of background, lifestyle, etc. Henry's research appears to confirm the conclusions of Bloom (1987: 25) that students are 'unified only in their relativism and their allegiance to equality'.

Bloom's (1987: 26) famous critique states that 'openness' is the only core virtue of modern students. He accuses American university professors of teaching students self-validation as opposed to self-examination and of promoting the idea that there is no truth, only 'lifestyles'. The purpose of higher education for Bloom is to create students who are aware of the vast array of possibilities that life offers and to be capable of choosing the good life. No such detailed analysis of the moral purposes of higher education has been undertaken recently in Britain, but would such an analysis be as pessimistic about student character as Bloom? Sir Walter Moberly's critique of

British higher education in 1949, entitled *The Crisis of the University*, is a strong precursor of Bloom, written forty years earlier. He says:

> Most students go through our universities without ever having been forced to exercise their minds on the issues which are really momentous. Under the guise of academic neutrality they are subtly conditioned to unthinking acquiescence in the social and political *status quo* and in a secularism on which they have never seriously questioned. Owing to the prevailing fragmentation of studies, they are not challenged to decide responsibility on a life-purpose or equipped to make such a decision wisely. They are not incited to disentangle and examine critically the assumptions and emotional attitudes underlying the particular studies they pursue, the profession for which they are preparing, the ethical judgements they are accustomed to make, and the political or religious convictions they hold. Fundamentally they are uneducated.

The above demonstrates that interpersonal sensibility, moral growth, a sense of social responsibility and intellectual toughness are all aspects of character that are at the core of being educated.

School to university

What are the lessons of school education for higher education? Citizenship education has been introduced to secondary schools and, in addition, 'education for character' is being promoted in schools by government. Universities cannot simply ignore the implications of these developments on their student body. These moral dimensions of education are clearly reflected in Section 2 (2) of the 1988 Education Reform Act, which states that all schools should promote the 'spiritual, moral, cultural, mental and physical development of pupils' together with preparing pupils 'for the opportunities, responsibilities and experiences of adult life'. Whilst these were the expressed aims of the whole curriculum, the Conservative government of the time made no statutory provision for values or civics education within it. The New Labour government in preparing the new National Curriculum 2000 for England sought to 'recognise a broad set of common values and purposes that underpin the school curriculum and the work of schools' (NC, 1999: 10). The government has accordingly been more forthright and explicit about the kinds of goals primary and secondary schools should follow by moving from guidance and discussion of school curriculum goals to a mandatory and 'official' rationale contained in the new National Curriculum (see Arthur, 2002).

New Labour has added to the National Curriculum in England by articulating new aims for schooling. In its Statement of Values, Aims and Purposes of the National Curriculum for England (1999: 10–11) the following is included: the development of children's social responsibility, community involvement, the development of effective relationships, knowledge and understanding of society, participation in the affairs of society, respect for others and the child's contribution to the building up of the common good. More specifically, the values that underpin the school curriculum are that education should reaffirm 'our commitment to the virtues of truth, justice, honesty, trust and a sense of duty'. The school curriculum should aim to 'develop principles for distinguishing between right and wrong', and pass on 'enduring values'. Whilst the document also encourages the promotion of 'self-esteem' and 'emotional well-being', the main thrust is the promotion of 'responsibility and rights'. New Labour also seeks to implement a policy of 'education with character', which it claims lies at the heart of its policies on education and citizenship.

Universities should also teach and challenge their students to make informed decisions, not only within academic disciplines but also in their personal lives concerning important questions of freedom, responsibility and ethics. Whilst the government has not directly involved itself in setting university education goals, universities cannot ignore what is happening in schools or the implications of New Labour's social inclusion agenda. For example, over the next three years universities will receive funding through The Higher Education Active Community Fund to promote social inclusion objectives by offering volunteering opportunities to students and staff alike. Some of these opportunities could lead to a re-discovery of character building activities in university life for many students and staff. For other universities it will reinforce the often uncelebrated community volunteering schemes that are already linked to a culture of good citizenship. Whilst it is not adequate to leave these things to the chance of a placement, it is a start.

Conclusion

It is possible to agree with Gellert (1981: 195) 'that in universities, as in other organisations, there are communicative and inter-actionist processes which go beyond the instrumental actions of research or the transmission and acquisition of knowledge. The acting individuals, in particular the student, are subject to effects of socialisation which shape their characters and personalities.' Whilst higher education institutions clearly exist for the education of their students, there is no guarantee today that they will consciously provide an environment for their full personal development. New universities at the beginning of the twentieth century consciously distanced themselves from religion, whilst at the same time providing space for religion as a 'private activity'. Character was still a concern, but a secular one emphasizing responsibility to society that was inspired more by Jowett than Newman. By the 1960s universities were increasingly defined as the 'instrumental' producers of the largest possible skilled output. Consequently, it became virtually impossible in terms of practicality (time/money) and ideology (universities for skills training) to prepare student characters adequately for a sense of duty to society. Many in the academic community are also disinclined to address ethical and character matters.

Each year increasing numbers of students enter higher education with a mixture of excitement and anticipation. Many, with their idealism, hope to shape themselves as whole human beings, both intellectually and morally in order to prepare for independent lives as citizens in the workforce. Some students seek to acquire a philosophy of life, others a better job. However, very few universities and colleges will have met their need for all-round development. Higher education has many opportunities to be a positive force in society and universities and colleges are beginning to look at student outcomes that concern public service and community involvement. Simply leaving the student to take responsibility for his or her own ethical development, on the basis that it is a matter of personal choice, may not promote the common good of society or the flourishing of the student if the university culture they experience is impoverished. The loss of time and space for many students in higher education limits their capacity and opportunity to become the human beings they ought to become. The person you become as a result of the total experience of being a student means that, as Carter (1980: 32–33) says, 'higher education should provide an all-round development, and not leave the fostering of qualities other than cognitive skills to chance'. The development of character or personal qualities must go beyond the 'corporate rhetoric' of the modern British university.

Since character development is not wholly a matter of private choice and higher education is not wholly neutral about conceptions of the good life, how should universities respond to questions of student character development? First, higher education must not react to increased demands for student character building because of some anxiety or fear about student behaviour. Fear must not be the justification for the provision of character building opportunities. Second, any response should be based on sound educational principles as opposed to political concerns. Academics today often do not want, or have so little time, to be role models or guardians for their students, but such a stance may convey the implicit message that the intellectual and practical are the only things that matter, that the moral and ethical are at best collateral, if not peripheral. Universities cannot assume that students will naturally evolve into ethically responsible people. Third, higher education needs to review or audit its fundamental core values in the context of its public duty to promote critical demo-cratic citizen students. This could be done by each institution of higher education describing the kind of students it seeks to develop and by outlining the overall philosophy that underlies its approach. From this philosophy or set of ideals it could also describe the kind of activities that offer the best opportunities of character development for its students. Fourth, higher education needs to review the various forms of its alliances with market forces that have so characterized university development in recent years. The 'corporate university' is having evermore obvious negative consequences for the character of students. Short-sighted profit interest in higher education may lead to a lack of context, which could mean that there is little point in cultivating character for nowhere in one's working life can one find good examples that character is of any particular importance. Perhaps these four points are simply too idealistic for contemporary universities to consider as serious options? Perhaps talk of the virtuous university is too far-fetched.

Ultimately, universities cannot teach what society and their own activity deny in practice. The producer ideology of skills mass production dominates university thinking and could be said to be irreconcilable with character education in any meaningful sense. Any initiatives by universities in character education have to be based on a national consensus which is necessarily so general that it can exert no specific influence on thought, let alone life. In contrast, the USA offers a range of private universities that have consciously opted out of the liberal consensus by offering a version of education not geared to skills outcomes. These universities are able to teach character and live it as a community of shared values. In Britain perhaps the only groups that may be able to contemplate such an independent university ideal in current conditions are religious groups such as Catholics, Evangelicals and Muslims. I would like to conclude with the suggestion that there is room for a university to be formally associated with a particular worldview and therefore ideal of character, so long as that worldview allows free critical discussion and is also genuinely a place of education and learning.

Chapter 3

Universities of character?

Charles L. Glenn

Can a 'real university' do anything to promote desirable character traits in its students, or would that be contrary to the openness that should characterize university life? Should there not be a vigorous debate, in a university, about whether there is such a thing as a perspective on the world that has sufficient validity to serve as a basis for attempting to develop, in students, a settled disposition to behave in 'virtuous' ways? Should not every such perspective be challenged, shown up as a mask for selfish interests? Is not it the teacher's role, like Socrates in the early dialogues, to leave his or her students less rather than more convinced of possessing the truth about particular virtues?

Lurking behind these questions is another, whether it is appropriate for a university to 'stand for' a particular way of understanding the world? Can it possibly be appropriate for a *university* (as contrasted with a liberal arts college on the American model) to have a distinctive character, an identity, which could serve as a basis for moral judgements?

By 'distinctive character of a university', I am obviously not referring to the fact that some are especially known for their history departments, while others have physics departments that attract enormous research grants. No, I mean the question in the sense in which the Free University in Amsterdam, for example, has sought to identify certain core values (whether or not derived from the distinctively Calvinist purpose for which it was founded) which do or could characterize its physics and its history departments alike.

It would be easy to respond that, of course, a university should 'stand for' free inquiry, tolerance and even celebration of differences, and of course those are very fine qualities, but in the last analysis they represent an uncertain trumpet which cannot quite bring itself to signal either advance or retreat. Free inquiry is most productive, after all, when it is in service to some pressing and deeply serious question. Scratching the itch of idle curiosity is a poor justification for the comfortable life of a scholar.

The answer to the first question depends to a great extent upon the answer that we give to the second. That is, a university which does not itself have a distinctive character is unlikely to be successful in developing character (in a different sense) in its students. Or, to be more accurate, it may tend only to develop in them a cynicism about the possibility of any universally valid standards that they should accept as binding.

For a university or other educational institution to have and to celebrate a distinctive character is not to turn it into a place of 'indoctrination', as we are so often warned. This has become one of those charges – like 'racism' and 'intolerance' – which can apparently be brought without the slightest need for evidence. Elmer John Thiessen points out that 'the distinction between true education and indoctrination is one of the most important educational distinctions to make', but that we should not allow a justified avoidance of indoctrination to force us into an approach to education which seeks to avoid advancing any consistent position other than indifferentism. There is no necessary conflict between foundational commitments and the ability to exercise critical judgments. What Thiessen calls 'normal rationality ... is sensitive to the need for human beings to have convictions, while at the same time recognizing the need for some degree of critical openness about these convictions. Normal rationality acknowledges that growth towards reflective, critical, and independent thought necessarily takes place within the context of "a convictional community" '.[1]

---

1. Elmer John Thiessen, *Teaching for Commitment*, Montreal: McGill-Queen's University Press, 1993, 18, 237.

The idea that a university could – even, perhaps, should – 'stand for something', and should in turn encourage its faculty and its students to consider a life of commitment, has become profoundly unfashionable in recent decades, which may be a good reason to take it out of the ashbin of history and consider it again.

Commonly, the claims of educational freedom are held to forbid any attempt to maintain a distinctive institutional character and to present that to students as worthy of serving as the basis of how they will approach the tasks of adult life. Educational freedom is taken to mean the freedom of each instructor to choose whether she will convey the subject matter of her teaching within a framework of meaning and, if so, what that framework will be. It is also taken to mean that university instruction is intended to shake whatever pre-conceptions students bring to their studies, and is thus essentially about *enlightenment*.

Let me stress that I am thoroughly convinced that teachers of young (and not-so-young) adults should do everything possible to develop in them the habits of critical thinking. But that does not have to mean that their education has to occur in a setting devoid of settled commitments. Nor does respect for the intellectual freedom of teachers require that every institution be indifferent to strongly held convictions.

Educational freedom (I will contend) *depends upon the freedom to shape – and (for individuals) to choose to study in or teach in – distinctive educational institutions. This implies an obligation upon faculty who have chosen to commit themselves to such an institution to teach in a way which engages positively with its educational project. Policies which provide scope and encouragement for schools and universities to represent distinctive and coherent viewpoints are an essential condition of educational freedom in a pluralistic society.*

Academic freedom

Academic freedom is generally understood to refer to the right of university faculty to follow their research wherever it leads them, and to teach their students on the basis of their own best understanding of the truth. Thus understood, it is a precious individual right to freedom of thought, painfully won against both overt and more subtle threats and, as such, recognized as having a significance which goes well beyond the interests of professors. As the United States Supreme Court pointed out in *Keyishian v. Board of Regents* 385 US 589 (1967), 'Our Nation is deeply committed to safeguarding academic freedom, which is of transcendent value to all of us and not merely to the teachers concerned. That freedom is therefore a special concern of the First Amendment [to the American *Constitution*], which does not tolerate laws that cast a pall of orthodoxy over the classroom.'

Academic freedom is not *only* an individual right, however; it is also a right sought or possessed by universities as institutions, the right to be self-governing with respect to academic matters. This right implies also the right to make academic decisions on the basis of a commitment to a particular viewpoint. A university need not be (though it may be) a sort of shopping mall of viewpoints which reflect nothing more than the diverse positions of its faculty.

For many – perhaps most in academic life – academic freedom requires that faculty make decisions about other faculty and the content of their instruction on the basis of criteria of academic excellence alone. A Catholic university thus has no obligation to ensure the orthodoxy of the teaching provided – even in theology – according to any external standard, including that of the church to which it claims a connection which has many material benefits Or so they say.

But what about secondary schools? Completely different, many would insist. As my friend and co-author Professor Jan De Groof wrote in one of his many books on education law, the secondary school 'teacher commits himself to an interpretation or clarification which is reconcilable with the educational project of the school's governing authority....Freedom of [school] ethos...in fact establishes limits at the time of assuming the position [of teacher]. In this way the teacher voluntarily accepts...limits upon his rights.'[2]

---

2. 'De leerkracht verbindt er zich toe voor de interpretatie of duiding die verenigbaar is met het opvoedingsproject van het schoolbestuur.... De vrijheid van richting... legt inderdaad beperkingen op van bij de toetreding tot het ambt. Daardoor aanvaardt de leerkracht vrijwillig... beperkingen op zijn rechten.' Jan De Groof and Paul Mahieu, *De school komt tot haar recht*, Leuven (Belgium): Garant, 1993, 28–29.

Schools that do not rest upon such a shared sense of mission are blown about by every wind. It would be bad enough if government made one set of demands, the economy another, parents a third, and teachers had their own goals and ways of understanding their responsibilities. But it is worse than that, since government gives a divided and conflicting message, the economy (in its varied sectors) is constantly sending different signals about what it wants, and parents and teachers vary enormously in their ways of thinking about education. And of course we must not forget the enormously diverse motivations and ambitions of pupils, despite what can seem their outward conformity to group norms.

The solution attempted in the United States, in the so-called comprehensive high school, has been to offer a little something for every interest, taste and ability. The diffuse – some say chaotic – curriculum offerings of large public secondary schools have been greatly criticized in recent years as leading to a 'Shopping Mall High School', which is, finally, not really able to educate in the full sense of that word. 'By promising to do everything well for everyone, educators have contributed to the growing sense that they can do nothing well for anyone... American schoolpeople have been singularly unable to think of an educational purpose that they should not embrace.'[3] This has led to a growing interest in variations on public education such as magnet schools and, more recently, charter schools with a distinctive and coherent educational mission to which both teachers and pupils are expected to adhere because of their voluntary participation.

Why should it be different at the university level? Is it simply because university students are assumed to be more mature, and thus do not need protection from the unorthodox opinions of their teachers? The American courts in recent years have found this distinction less and less convincing, concluding that students at the secondary level are quite capable of making up their minds and resisting the ideas and perspectives proposed to them in school. And do not university students have considerable freedom to avoid institutions whose religious or philosophical character seem to them a smothering

---

3. Arthur G. Powell, Eleanor Farrar and David K. Cohen, *The Shopping Mall High School*, Boston: Houghton Mifflin, 1985, 305.

orthodoxy? What is there really to fear, with respect to the freedom of conscience of students, from universities which maintain and promote a distinctive ethos?

The argument for academic freedom, however, is not ordinarily made in terms of the intellectual freedom of students (unless as a rhetorical device) but of the scholarly integrity of professors. Surely they should not be subjected to any limits on their freedom of investigation, to the boldness of the questions that they raise and the unorthodoxy of the answers that they offer, or limits other than those defining scholarly integrity!

There can be no question that the conditions, in the early nineteenth century, out of which arose the doctrine of *Lehrfreiheit* justified this claim of intellectual independence. New advances in methods of conducting research and the questioning of received knowledge occurred – not by accident – at a time when both Protestant and Catholic orthodoxy seemed intellectually exhausted and were clinging as a result all the more stubbornly to authority over the universities. It was in this context and at this historical moment that the insistence of the very small elite of university professors on their right to pursue knowledge *in their specializations* wherever it led them had its moral justification.

This principle continues to apply, though as Nisbet wrote during the academic turmoil of thirty years ago, 'It was one thing to tolerate the idea of academic freedom when it meant only a physicist's or sociologist's right to write and teach *as a physicist or sociologist*. It is something very different when the idea is applied indiscriminately to all aspects of existence.'[4]

Something very different is at stake in today's mass higher education. In 1869, there were 5553 faculty in higher education institutions in the United States; in 1999 there were more than a million, nearly 600,000 of them full-time. It is not surprising that, by all accounts, the majority of this army of faculty members pursue no significant research interests beyond their often *pro forma* dissertations or the receipt of

---

4. Robert A. Nisbet, *The Degradation of the Academic Dogma: The University in America, 1945–1970*, New York: Basic Books, 1971, 61.

tenure and have only the most conventional opinions within their own fields.

We must not exaggerate; there are of course tens of thousands of university faculty, in the United States as in Europe, who manage to combine lively intellectual pursuits with engaging and useful teaching – indeed, the latter is unlikely to be sustained for long without the former. Their investigations and speculations must be protected, lest the life of the mind wither and, with it, the vitality of our universities. *Within their area of competence*, it is important to subject them only to the discipline of peer review on the basis of scholarly standards. Expecting a university-level teacher of – say – literature to avoid imposing upon students his uninformed opinions about religious and moral questions which conflict with the 'educational project' of the institution which employs him does not prevent him from being as unorthodox as he wishes about the authorship of the plays usually attributed to Shakespeare. Of course he has a right to freedom of speech on any matter on which he chooses to entertain an opinion, but only in his capacity as citizen and not in his capacity as teacher and with a 'captive audience' of students.

The threatened freedom of universities

The American Association of University Professors insists that 'the professor does not speak for the institution, nor the institution for the professor'.[5] In fact, the distinction suggested is by no means so clear. For most students, in fact, the professor *is* the university, at least with respect to matters which the professor chooses to raise in her lectures. Before we can explore further the academic freedom of individual teachers, it is important to consider the academic freedom of educational institutions.

The earliest universities were under Church sponsorship and supported by private and ecclesiastical endowments as well as by

5. Alan Charles Kors and Harvey A. Silverglate, *The Shadow University: The Betrayal of Liberty in America's Campuses*, The Free Press, 1998, 57.

student fees. One of the early forms of government involvement was the recognition of degrees granted by certain universities, which gave them a monopoly position. Since government was, with the Church, the major employer of university graduates, this was a major but indirect form of support. Thus a royal writ of 1334 referred to 'the King's universities' of Oxford and Cambridge, though in fact the universities were self-governing within the broad jurisdiction of Church officials.[6]

The autonomy of universities is, arguably, more in question today, now that most – in Europe at least – derive their financial support primarily from government. This has led a British historian to insist that 'it has become necessary to reassert the medieval idea of liberties, to argue that Universities have their own independent sphere of judgement, in which the State should not meddle'.[7]

Financial dependence did not develop overnight, of course; Nisbet traces the elaboration of a theory of academic freedom to the growing role of the German states in relation to their universities.

> What the German professors said, in effect, was: the university can no longer be the privileged enclave it has been since the Middle Ages; but even though the power of ultimate direction of finance has been taken over by the government ministry, we, the professors, reaffirm our historic right to autonomy in academic matters.[8]

The extent of government funding of universities has grown enormously since World War II, in Europe as in the United States, with inevitable consequences for their real autonomy. Russell's warning could be made equally well about the situation in other western societies that 'the almost total dependence of British universities on the State for the funding of their basic operations has for a long time left them dangerously vulnerable to the power of the State'.[9] Decisions continue to be made by university faculty, but it is within the context

---

6. Conrad Russell, *Academic Freedom*, London: Routledge, 1993.
7. Ibid., 3.
8. Nisbet, 61.
9. Russell, 7.

of budgetary policy-making that, over time, can leave them arguing over trifles. This has led to the familiar quip that the reason faculty meetings are so contentious is that the issues are so unimportant!

Nor is the situation very different in the private universities which play such an important role in the United States and Japan. More even than in Europe, it is essential for them to respond to a market – to what students believe worth their while to study. Max Weber wrote, eighty years ago, that 'the German universities…are engaged in a most ridiculous competition for enrollments';[10] if only he had lived to see the glossy promotional packages that come in each day's mail to American high school seniors from universities thousands of miles away!

Ironically, the combined pressures of government and the student market represent little threat to intellectual independence – professors are free to express the goofiest ideas without fear of bureaucratic retaliation or a drop in applications – but have the effect of rendering the intellectual enterprise increasingly marginal. It is no accident that, in recent decades, much of the generation and play of new ideas in the United States, at least, has occurred in off-campus 'think tanks' (more politely, policy institutes) and journals, not in university faculty lounges.

In both public and private universities, then, whether to build a strong programme in Byzantine studies is not simply a faculty decision to be made on the basis of the excellence of the research available and yet to be done, but responds to market pressures either directly or by mediation through government decisions. Parenthetically, some of the stranger twists of scholarly emphasis in the humanities may owe more to a perception of what will 'sell' to students than to genuine ideological conviction on the part of faculty. Giving a feminist or 'Queer Studies' twist to one's scholarly work may bring in new cohorts of students and help to keep a department afloat!

But government and market pressures do not have to translate into loss of the distinctive character of a university, if we mean by that

---

10. 'Science as a vocation' (*Wissenschaft als Beruf*, 1919), in H. H. Gerth and C. Wright Mills, editors and translators, *From Max Weber: Essays in Sociology*, New York: Oxford University Press, 1946, 133.

its ethos as expressed in the flavour which it gives to its instruction as well as its life as a community. In fact, I think it probable that the ability of a university to retain a significant degree of operational autonomy in decisions which shape the education it provides is directly related to the insistence with which it holds onto a clearly stated mission. Government officials – and I served in that much-maligned capacity for twenty one years – tend to push in where there is no coherent resistance. Generally they have no stomach for conflict with opponents who can articulate clearly their reasons for opposing specific external mandates. That, in fact, is a central conclusion of my research on the effects of government funding on faith-based institutions in Europe and the United States. I found support in political scientist Stephen Monsma's survey of colleges, social agencies and international aid organizations; those whose religious identity is clearly profiled, Monsma found, report *less* trouble with government than do those which have become unclear about their identity.[11]

Nor is this simply a psychological effect; there is extensive legislation and jurisprudence in several European countries as well as in the United States which grants a higher protection to the autonomy of educational institutions in matters which affect their distinctive character.[12]

Clarity of identity also plays an important role in dealing with the market forces which have such an enormous impact upon universities in the United States and, to an increasing extent, in Europe. Higher education institutions are inclined to seek to improve their market position by blurring their distinctiveness in an effort to appeal more broadly, but this often proves a mistake. 'Generic brands' tend not to do well in marketplace competition, especially when what is at stake is as expensive and as consequential as higher education.

In short, the possession of some guiding purpose apart from responding to government dictation and market forces is itself an important shield against both. 'A liberty, in the medieval sense', after all, 'was no more than an enclave, a corporate autonomy in society

---

11. Stephen V. Monsma, *When Sacred and Secular Mix*, Lanham (MD): Rowman and Littlefield, 1996.
12. See Glenn, *The Ambiguous Embrace: Government and Faith-based Schools and Social Agencies*, Princeton University Press, 2000.

that deserved its own freedom to act in proportion to the honor of its mission'. An educational institution without its own distinctive mission is compelled to accept whatever missions are imposed upon it by society. 'If the university rides off in all directions at once, it will hardly go anywhere.'[13]

Character in universities

Educational institutions need to learn to avoid the common assumption that there are two spheres of knowledge, one of the factual world and the other of values. To accept Max Weber's separation between spheres of facts-without-values and values-without-facts is fatal to creating the kinds of schools and universities that are needed, because it suggests the possibility of adding on elements of moral teaching or character development as a supplement to the fundamental instructional programme. The entire programme of instruction in subject matter should be undertaken in a way that contributes to the development of character and an understanding of the world, which will lead to responsible adulthood.

This does not mean that a little flavouring, a little sauce of some religious or ethical tradition, should be poured over every subject, but rather that in the entire teaching enterprise there should be a fundamental seriousness about raising the important questions and addressing them from the perspective of a consistent framework of values and convictions. Specifically, when issues of worldview are being discussed, they should be discussed in relation to the competencies that students are developing and not as a separate and otherworldly set of concerns. By the same token, when competencies are being developed and discussed, there should also be consideration of how and why they are being developed and for what purposes they will be used.

Institutional organization and daily interactions are primary in shaping not only the climate but also the very character of a college or university, the explicit way in which its life and mission are presented

---

13. Nisbet, 61, 135.

both externally and internally. This is not to say that we should minimize the importance of either the curriculum or its pedagogical and organizational dimensions. The three elements together make up the institution's distinctive character or identity. In a coherent college, a shared worldview informs the curriculum and is expressed in the relationships of professors and students and of professors with one another.

There is thus no such thing as a model of what a Protestant, Catholic, Muslim, Jewish, or Humanist university should be like. Each must find its own specific way of combining these elements in a form that reflects the understandings and commitments of those participating. What is essential is that these understandings and commitments not be inconsistent with one another; they need to reinforce each other, rather than be in conflict. It is unfortunately by no means always the case that colleges calling themselves Christian, for example, in fact consciously and effectively work to develop a unity of these three components of their life and mission. The identity should not be seen as simply an add-on, but as a fundamental vision working its way through all that the institution does.

Does not that describe the fundamental convergence which would make any educational institution – including a university – coherent and effective? And is not that a good working definition of academic freedom as it applies to institutional autonomy? And would not a university manifesting such coherence be in strong competitive position?

The research about motivations for *school* choice, in Europe and the United States, shows that many parents choose faith-based schools for their children who do not themselves share that faith. They do so, apparently, out of a well-founded sense that purposeful schools, possessing what has been called 'integrative capital', provide good education. These are schools that 'are unified, disciplined, and consistent in what they expect of adults and offer students'. By contrast, 'weak and less coherent schools are hesitant to impose expectations that . . . students or interest group representatives object to. Most are reluctant to engage topics that can become controversial and often content themselves with formulaic celebrations of ethnic and cultural customs. Stronger, more coherent schools regard diversity as a topic of respectful but serious conversation, not a source of distinctive rights. They do not translate differences in student background into differences in expectations for learning, effort, or behavior.'[14]

While there are of course many distinctions between schools and universities, this description of weak schools sounds uncomfortably close to the reality of many higher education institutions, and that of schools with 'integrative capital' identifies characteristics possessed by effective colleges and universities. The latter tend to be 'unified, disciplined, and consistent', not blown about by every pressure from the surrounding environment.

Ethos cannot substitute for academic excellence, but the continuing popularity of Protestant and Catholic schools in the Netherlands suggests that the widespread secularization in Dutch society has not abated the demand for education shaped by a clearly defined and distinctive mission.[15]

I anticipate the objection that a university should not, by affirming a distinctive character, contribute to the division of society into competing philosophical camps; that its mission is to allow all the voices to be heard in a rich symphony. As Edward Reisner pointed out more than eighty years ago, however, the existence of institutions that are coherent around a particular understanding of education is not inconsistent with an overall diversity of ideas and an open debate about issues of fundamental importance, so long as the society supports institutional pluralism.

There has been in our country a tendency for individual colleges to control rather narrowly the instruction given within their classrooms and to censor the personal conduct of teachers and students according to a rigid standard. Such '*Lehr-und-Lern-freiheit*' [freedom to teach and to learn] as has existed in our country has come about rather through the multiplicity of educational foundations with their wide variety of purposes and beliefs. Whom the denominational college has cast out for utterances at variance with its canon some state college or university has welcomed for his vigorous intellect; and whom the state university has cast out for unacceptable political or economic

---

14. Paul T. Hill and Mary Beth Celio, *Fixing Urban Schools*, Washington, DC: Brookings Institution Press, 1998.
15. See the extended discussion in *Verzuiling in het onderwijs*, edited by Dijkstra, Dronkers and Hofman, Groningen: Wolters-Noordhoff, 1997.

teachings, some private institution has gathered to its boson with honor and affection. The result has been a degree of intellectual independence and freedom, when the nation as a whole is considered, that has been of inestimable value in the development of science and the enrichment of public life.[16]

In an unconscious echo of Reisner, Thiessen concludes that 'the best guarantee against institutional indoctrination is that there be a plurality of institutions'.[17]

Why should a particular tradition be privileged over others by a college or university? Not because of any claim to unique authority or unique access to truth, which would be inappropriate in a pluralistic society, but because perspectives, angles on the truth, need to be nurtured in friendly soil. If, as often happens in classes and discussions, religious viewpoints are ruled out *a priori*, there is no chance that they will be nurtured to the point that they can enter fully into the exchange at a level appropriate to the search for truth. Not only is the faith of the student either withered or stunted at the level of unreflecting childish sentiment, but the wide-ranging discussion which is the essence of university life is impoverished as a result. As one of the wisest observers of the culture of universities has observed, 'With a naivete matching that of many believers, the secularist critics of religious belief have sometimes proceeded as though assumptions a priori that cannot be proven were exclusively the property of believers, and therefore as if their [own] scholarship and their university were free of presuppositions.'[18]

In fact, it is fair to ask whether the 'pluralistic university' is as open to divergent viewpoints as the rhetoric assumes. Historian George Marsden has pointed out that 'pluralism as it is often conceived of today seems to be almost a code word for its opposite, a new expression of the melting-pot ideal. Persons from a wide variety of races and cultures are welcomed into the university, but only on the condition that they think more-or-less alike.'[19]

---

16. Edward H. Reisner, *Nationalism and Education since 1789*, New York: Macmillan, 1922, 363.
17. Thiessen, 274.
18. Jaroslav Pelikan, *The Idea of the University – A Reexamination*, New Haven and London: Yale University Press, 1992, 47.
19. George M. Marsden, *The Soul of the American University: From Protestant Establishment to Established Nonbelief*, New York: Oxford University Press, 1994, 432.

In effect, a secularist orthodoxy places limits on intellectual life which are, in their own way, as hostile to academic freedom as were the religious orthodoxies of the eighteenth century. As a result, 'a professed "knowledge" about human life and society, about human history and culture, that is as ignorant about the faith-dimension as is much of the current scholarship of humanists and social scientists in many universities…is fundamentally deficient – deficient as knowledge and as scholarship, completely apart from what it may or may not mean for the life of faith.'[20]

The danger today, surely, is not that religious viewpoints will impose themselves tyrannically, but that they will be so excluded from the ongoing discussion by which truth is discovered that – even in universities with a religious identity – they will make no contribution. It is unimaginable that, in a university at the turn of the millennium, a religious orthodoxy could obtain the stranglehold that 'multiculturalism' (the ideology, not the sociological reality) has acquired in many of the best American universities. According to well-placed observers, there is now

> only one appropriate set of views about race, gender, sexual preference, and culture, and holding an inappropriate belief, once truth has been offered, is not an intellectual disagreement, but an act of oppression or denial. All behavior and thought are 'political', including opposition to politicized 'awareness' workshops. The goal of such opposition is [assumed to be] the continued oppression of women and of racial or sexual minorities.[21]

Can anyone imagine a specific religious doctrine coming to have equal authority at a distinguished university today?

What individual academic freedom requires

But what about individual academic freedom? And does not it necessarily come into conflict with a university which is seeking to

---

20. Pelikan, 39.
21. Kors and Silverglate, 215.

maintain or reclaim a distinctive character? I am going to suggest that freedom for the individual professor, at least in her capacity as a teacher, depends at least in part upon a collective freedom, that of the institution of which she is a constitutive member rather than an employee.

Teaching is not a solitary enterprise. We do it in the company not only of our students but of others who have taught and are teaching and will teach them – an invisible presence, to be sure, but none the less essential and subtly influential. Medieval universities were corporate bodies of professors who could take for granted, in large measure, a common worldview and a common faith, who joined at great occasions in common liturgies – how difficult it is today, in a great university, to persuade the faculty to come together for *any* occasion! It was not that they did not disagree; on the contrary, it was precisely what they held in common that permitted their debates to be so lively and so frequently productive. It is an impoverishment of the modern university that we find it hard to disagree on important matters because we hold so little in common intellectually. We have no common ground on which to meet, even to quarrel.

Surely the freedom of a professor to teach, really to teach, is enhanced if he can teach within a shared framework of meaning, sustained by what colleagues have taught and will teach.

I am emphatically *not* saying that tests of orthodoxy are necessary or desirable in a university, but suggesting that commitment to a shared *ethos*, an understanding of what is ultimately important, would contribute measurably to the real freedom of faculty in their capacity as teachers. If our teaching is too often timid, that is because it does not take place within such a shared ethos, so that we are forced constantly to assess whether and to what extent we can raise the deepest questions, call upon our students to stretch their minds, to think about the relationship of our subject – whatever it may be – to questions of ultimate purpose and meaning.

Speaking boldly of such matters, not to indoctrinate but to challenge, is surely one of the essentials of effective teaching. It can occur only in a setting where there is a shared understanding that such questions are legitimate and important. 'Education for life' is surely what we who love to teach think that we are about. Not that this reduces to the slightest degree our obligation to the truth and to the discipline of our academic subject. Our contribution to shaping the lives and the character of our students is not achieved by preaching to them, but by the humility and attention with which we search for the truth and share with them both the process and the results.

'Humility and attention' – I owe the phrase to my Boston University colleague, the poet Geoffrey Hill, who thus describes how the poet stands before reality, but it could be applied just as appropriately to the work of a scientist, of an art historian, of a psychologist. I was particularly struck, at the session of the *Waardenproject* of the Free University in Amsterdam, in September 1997, with the description of the respectful attention which the Biology Faculty sought to develop in its students, towards the nature of research, towards laboratory animals, towards human beings who will be affected by their work.

This is why 'post-modernism' is so destructive of a central value of the university's mission, with its mocking detachment from the search for truth. This is also why the exaltation of 'theory' in the humanities has succeeded in chasing away so many students who simply love poetry or novels for the direct experience of reality which they offer the attentive reader. And this is why, finally, we cannot accept Weber's famous claim that *Wissenschaft* must be value-free.

It is a false accusation, which we have been too ready to accept, on the part of those who mock rooted convictions that 'real science' cannot be done by believers, that faith imposes a darkness on the mind. If we reflect for a moment we know that is not true, that the posture of 'humility and attention', which is essential to all real scholarship and all real teaching, are virtues precisely nurtured by a life of faith. Of course there are many religious people, as there are many secularists, who lack those virtues, but this is the result of personal shallowness and not of the convictions that they hold. William James correctly saw that many religious people approach life's challenges with enthusiasm and engagement, not with the blinkered narrowness of which they are accused by their secularist mockers.

Surely there is a place, in a pluralistic society, for universities where the outer limits of inquiry are pressed with that enthusiasm and engagement, with that humility and attention, which are an integral part of the Christian approach to life. Surely there is a place for teaching which is coherent and mutually reinforcing, while avoiding any sort of indoctrination. And surely it can only strengthen a university to define a common ground of core values which relate it to a tradition of serious engagement with ideas. Nothing could be more foolish than to accept the historical inevitability of the continued secularization of thought, or to assume that the ideas which previous generations of honest seekers after truth and justice held could no longer help us in our search for truth and for justice today.

Chapter 4

Community, service learning and higher education in the UK

John Annette

Introduction

Why is there an increasing interest in community and community involvement in the UK? In considering community primarily in terms of the ideas of communitarianism (Frazer, 1999a; Arthur, 2000), I want to analyse what role it can play in developing an education for democratic citizenship in higher education. This challenge to higher education in the UK to provide curriculum innovation which can encourage undergraduates to develop the values of social responsibility through volunteering will be seen in the context of the rethinking of higher education which has followed from the 'Dearing Commission' review of UK higher education. This will also involve examining whether or not 'service learning' or 'community-based learning' can provide a basis for constructing curriculum innovations which can provide learning for democratic citizenship in higher education. This will involve considering the growth of service learning in the USA and in the UK where its recent development has been influenced by US higher education. Finally, I want to consider what challenges this provides for the future of higher education in the UK.

In contemporary political thinking the concept of community has become both philosophically and 'politically' significant. Community has also become increasingly the focus of government policy in the UK and the USA. From the 'Third-Way' communitarianism of New Labour or the New Democrats to the emergence of communitarian Compassionate Conservatism, the idea of community is now seen as a key to rethinking the relationship between civil society and the state. Government social policy concerning neighbourhood renewal and urban renaissance stresses the role of citizens in inner-city areas in designing and rebuilding their communities (Sirianni and Friedland, 2001; Taylor, 2003). The Neighbourhood Renewal Programme of the Office of the Deputy Prime Minister calls for new ideas on community enterprise, community safety, healthy communities, sustainable communities and learning communities.

According to the UK Home Secretary, David Blunkett, 'Our challenge today is to provide a meaningful sense of belonging and community engagement, which can be both robust and adaptable in the face of wider change' (Blunkett, 2001: 22).

Linked to this challenge is the perceived sense of the loss of community in contemporary British society. This lost sense of community also underlies the idea of social capital, which has recently been popularized by Robert Putnam in his study of the decline of civic engagement and social capital in the USA (Putnam, 2000). The concept of social capital has provided a theoretical basis for understanding the importance of community, which according to the neo-Tocquevillian analysis of Robert Putnam and his colleagues has important consequences for citizenship and political participation. While Putnam and others have analysed the decline of traditional volunteering in the USA, it is interesting to note that in the UK there has been a much smaller decline (Hall, 2002).

In contemporary political and sociological theory there has been a renewed interest in the idea of community (Bauman, 2000; Delanty, 2003). The concept of community is an elastic concept which allows for an enormous range of meanings. From virtual communities to imaginary communities there are conceptual understandings of community to be found in a wide range of traditions of thought and academic disciplines. I would argue that there are at least four main ways of conceptualizing community. (There are a number of contemporary writers who offer alternative ways of representing the varying understandings of the meaning of community; cf. Frazer, 1999a; Nash, 2002; Delanty, 2003; Taylor, 2003.) The first is to consider community descriptively as a place or neighbourhood. Thus the government's Neighbourhood Renewal Strategy talks of revitalizing communities primarily in terms of neighbourhoods. The second is to talk of community as a normative ideal linked to respect, solidarity and inclusion, which can be found in the now well-established debate between liberalism and its communitarian critics (Mulhall and Swift, 1996). The third way of understanding community is based on the construction of cultural identities and can be found in communities of 'interest'. This conception is based on a politics of identity and recognition of difference. The fourth way is to consider community as a political ideal which is linked to participation, involvement and citizenship, especially on the level of the community.

It is the case, of course, that these conceptual understandings of community are often elided and combined to produce hybrid conceptualizations of contemporary community. Thus a political understanding of community may be based in a specific neighbour-hood where there are public places and may include a variety of communities of identity or interest. It is also the case that political communitarianism can be understood through the analysis of the politics of community in terms of liberalism, communitarianism or civic republicanism. Advocates of both communitarianism and civic republicanism have recently begun to revive the idea of a civic service linked to the ideal of service to the local community. In Britain, James McCormick in a pamphlet on 'Citizen's Service', for the Institute For Public Policy Research (1994), argued for a national voluntary Citizen's Service initiative (McCormick, 1994), and more recently in the USA there has been a renewed interest in establishing a form of national service which would build on the success of the Americorps programme of the Corporation for National Service (Gorham, 1992; Dionne, Jr *et al.*, 2003). Susan Stroud on the basis of her previous work for the Corporation and the Ford Foundation has been exploring this theme internationally (Gorham, 1992; McCormick, 1994). To what extent has this communitarian concern for civic service influenced the curriculum of higher education?

Higher education reform in the UK

In what way has the rethinking of higher education in the UK created the opportunity to provide for undergraduates as part of the curriculum an education for democratic citizenship? In 1997 a major Royal Commission under Lord Dearing was established to examine the future of British higher education. One of the main aims of higher education, according to the Dearing Report on NICHE (1997), is to contribute to a democratic, civilized and inclusive society. The emphasis on civic engagement highlights the need for the curriculum in higher education to prepare graduates to become active citizens and to participate not only in formal politics but also play a leadership role in civil society.

In the UK this is particularly a challenge for higher education as the new citizenship curriculum in schools, following on from the Crick Report on Education for Citizenship and the Teaching of Democracy in Schools in 1998, has resulted in the establishment of service learning programmes increasingly in UK secondary or high schools (Advisory Group on Citizenship, 1998; Annette, 2000; Potter, 2002).

The 'Dearing Report' (NICHE, 1997) follows on from an increasing range of work done since the 1970s which has emphasized the importance in higher education of the development of what has been termed transferable, personal, core or key skills (Drew, 1998). The challenge for higher education, according to the Dearing Report, is to provide an academic framework that is based on the acquisition of critical knowledge, which is mostly structured around the present framework established by the academic disciplines, and which provides students with the opportunity to develop essential key skills and capabilities. This emphasis on learning not only for academic knowledge but also for key skills and capabilities, including student leadership, can also be found in the USA in the work of Ernest Boyer and the Carnegie Foundation and more recently in the writings of Thomas Ehrlich (Ehrlich *et al.*, 2000; Ehrlich *et al.*, 2003). It is being increasingly recognized that an important way in which students can develop key skills through work experience and also experience an education for citizenship is through service learning or community-based learning.

Higher education in Britain is rapidly becoming a mass system, perhaps on the model of the USA. With a participation rate approaching 45 per cent the Higher Education system in Britain now faces the challenge of the White Paper (2003) 'The Future of Higher Education' and the implications of the upgrading of the status and role of further education. According to Peter Scott, 'the result is a disjunction, even a paradox. British Higher Education has become a mass system in its public structures, but remains an elite one in its private instincts' (Scott, 1995: 2). The development of the mass system of higher education in the USA began in the 1960s during a period of sustained economic growth and an optimistic political age. In Britain, its development in the 1990s has been against a background of scepticism and uncertainty.

The rise of the 'multiversity' began in the 1960s and, according to Clark Kerr, it is made up of many academic departments and institutes, where the totality of the whole is organized on the pragmatic principles of administrative convenience. The multiversity was seen as crucially producing and reproducing knowledge through the semi-autonomous activities of its professors, departments, institutes, colleges and faculties. For A. H. Halsey, this whole process of change in Britain has resulted in what he terms 'the decline of donnish dominion' (Halsey, 1995). Yet the process should not be seen as a simple linear one, nor determined by the American model. Much of the literature of the subject has either focused on the history of changing institutional forms and systems or emphasized the university as a mainly research-oriented institution. The academic study of the higher education curriculum, however, raises some important questions about how we can understand the changing nature of the higher education system. These changes rather than being viewed as a threat to academic standards or even academic freedom can also be seen as a process of integrating the university into democratic society. Recently, Thomas Ehrlich of the Carnegie Foundation has edited a collection of essays on the civic responsibility of higher education where models of higher education community partnerships, especially in research universities, are explored (Ehrlich, 2000).

In many recent studies of higher education the specialization of academic disciplines has been seen as one of the main factors in the disappearance of a common academic community. According to the

Carnegie Commission Report on the Undergraduate Experience in America, 'Too many campuses, we found, are divided by narrow departmental interest that become obstacles to learning in a richer sense. Students and faculty, like passengers on a airplane, are members of a community of convenience' (Boyer, 1987: 84). Professor Ron Barnett in his study of the idea of higher education has written, 'So, a key curriculum question in higher education is this: Can a discipline based curriculum fulfil the wider objectives, objectives which call for individual disciplines to be transcended? Can a programme of studies which is organised around a particular discipline, engender an understanding of its limitations, and indeed a place in the total map of knowledge?' (Barnett, 1990: 177; Bender and Schorske, 1997; Beecher, 2003). The question of what will be the future of academic disciplines is a complicated one.

According to the anthropologist Clifford Geertz, there has been a 'blurring of genres' as academic disciplines as interpretive communities seek to establish new configurations for the organization of the production and reproduction of academic knowledge, and in doing so begin to move across disciplinary boundaries. While academic disciplines may provide obstacles to rethinking the curriculum, they could also provide the possibility of producing new interdisciplinary and multidisciplinary perspectives from within their disciplinary configurations. The development of a key skills curriculum in higher education might possibly lead to a reconfiguration of the map of academic knowledge and a change to the dominance of the academic disciplines. The challenge facing the academic disciplines is how they will respond to these changes by not only rethinking the teaching and assessment practices within the disciplines but also contributing to the discussion about what a key skills curriculum might be for undergraduate education.

The increasing emphasis in the 'Dearing Report on Higher Education in the Learning Society' on the organization and outcomes of the learning experiences of students and the achievement of key skills and capabilities (and not just subject-based knowledge as the aim of a higher education) is part of the post-Dearing debate about what will be the future of higher education in Britain. The Dearing Report 'endorses the value of some exposure of the student to the wider world as part of a programme of study'. And it states that, 'This may be achieved through work experience, involvement in student union activities, or in work in community or voluntary settings' (NICHE, 1997, Section 9.26). It is in this context that I would like to now examine some ways in which learning through volunteering or service learning has been introduced into Higher Education in the USA since the late 1980s and more recently in the UK.

Service learning or community-based learning

An important way in which students can develop key skills through work experience and experience an education for citizenship is through service learning or community-based learning as it is better known in the UK. Service learning involves students working in partnership with local communities and learning through a structured programme of learning which includes reflection on the learning.

At the core of community service learning is the pedagogy of experiential learning, which is based on the thought of John Dewey and more recently David Kolb *et al*. In the USA the National Society for Experiential Education (NSEE) has since 1971 been engaged in the development of and research into experiential education, and more recently the American Association of Higher Education (AAHE), in partnership with the Corporation for National Service, has commissioned volumes by leading academic figures to examine the importance of service learning in higher education. What is impressive about the work of the NSEE and the AAHE is that not only is there research done on pedagogic practices but also, going beyond anecdotal evidence, there is research into the evaluation of the learning outcomes of service learning. One of the leading research projects into the learning outcomes of service learning has been published as 'Where's the Learning in Service Learning?' by Janet Eyler and Dwight Giles (Eyler and Giles, 1999). What is important about community service learning is that it is multi-disciplinary and can be integrated into a wide variety of academic disciplines and learning experiences. These could include environmental and global study and the opportunity for students to undertake community service learning while studying abroad, especially through the EU-funded Socrates network. There are available links with universities with service learning programmes in the USA, South Africa, Jordan, Mexico, Australia, etc. (cf. Annette, 2003a). Community service learning can be established generically across a university but a major challenge facing universities will be to encourage disciplinary and multidisciplinary community service learning in the subject-based curriculum.

An interesting feature of service learning in the USA is the importance of service learning in many of the faith-based higher education institutions and especially at Christian universities and colleges (Devine Favazza and McLain, 2002; Heffner and Beversluis, 2003; Hesser, 2003). From Catholic social teaching to the Protestant social gospel there are a variety of ways in which faith traditions influence the understandings of service and moral and social responsibility as well as character development within the service learning programmes in Christian higher education institutions. In the UK, James Arthur in his important study of the communitarian agenda in education argues that many faith schools are based on a 'religious communitarianism'. He also argues that this is particularly true of Catholic schools given the Catholic Church's 'social teachings' (Arthur, 2000), and following Paul Valley he argues that this social teaching is inherently communitarian (Vallely, 1998). It is interesting to note that the Muslim Council of Great Britain (MCB) in its inaugural meeting in 1997 used the theme 'Seeking the Common Good', which was based on the document produced by the Catholic Bishops of England and Wales, 'The Common Good and the Catholic Church's Social Teachings', published a year earlier. The impressive book *The Politics of Hope* of the Chief Rabbi Jonathan Sacks, first published in 1997, also represents a religious communitarianism.

James Arthur also argues that there are some key distinctions that can be made between a secular communitarianism and a religious one and that for many faith schools it is impossible for them to be based on a secular communitarianism. Referring to the work of Robert Bellah with its references to religions as 'communities of memory', Arthur argues that the secular communitarian advocacy of a 'civic religion' has an instrumental view of religion as serving the public good, which takes priority over the transcendent purpose of religion. It is clearly this civic role of religion, however, which has influenced New Labour's policy of supporting faith-based community action and is the encouragement for the development of faith schools. There is considerable evidence of an increase in faith-based community action in both the UK and the USA since the 1980s. It was in 1985 that the Archbishop of Canterbury's Commission on Urban Priority Areas published its report 'Faith in the City' (Archbishop of Canterbury, 1985). This report followed on from the Brixton race riots and the report of Lord Scarman's enquiry and it emphasized the social responsibility of the church for its poor inner city communities. Subsequently the Church Urban League was established (Lawless *et al.*, 1998) and the Urban Theology Group was formed in 1990 and has continued to reflect on the theological implications of urban poverty (Northcott, 1998).

More recently there has been a growing number of studies of the role of faith communities in urban regeneration in the UK (Farnell, 2001; Farnell *et al.*, 2003; Lukka and Locke with Soteri-Procter, 2003). As faith-based colleges of higher education play an increasingly important role in UK higher education, it will be interesting to see whether or not religious communitarianism will influence them to develop service learning programmes which enable their students to develop a distinctive approach to learning and working with community partners.

The provision of the opportunity for students to participate in community service learning also requires partnerships with the university's local communities (Jacoby, 2003). It is interesting to note that the CVCP report on 'Universities and Communities' (1994) highlights the role of universities in local and regional development but, except for the appendix by John Mohan, it does not consider how university and community partnerships will impact upon the curriculum of higher education (CVCP, 1994; Elliott *et al.*, 1996). The increasing recognition of the need to provide students with the opportunities to develop key skills and capabilities in higher education, in order to prepare them for lifelong learning, should hopefully encourage academics to consider how learning in the community will best provide such learning experiences.

It should also encourage them to examine how the delivery of the curriculum will best meet the needs of local communities (Watson and Taylor, 1998). This emphasis on partnership working with local communities is especially true of those who advocate learning through community-based research (Hall and Hall, 2002; Jacoby, 2003; cf. Strand *et al.*, 2003). There is also an increasing emphasis on the need for service learning programmes to meet the needs of local community partners (Jacoby, 2003). There is also a new challenge to engage in research to better understand the learning and wider moral and civic outcomes for students, universities and the local communities from service learning (Gelmon *et al.*, 2001). An important research question which needs to be examined is, what are the necessary elements of a service learning programme which can build not only social capital but also active citizenship (Campbell, 2000; Kahne *et al.*, 2000; Ehrlich *et al.*, 2003; Annette, 2003b).

Service learning in the USA

In the USA there has since the 1960s been a tradition of service learning based upon the principles of experiential education which has been supported by the National Society for Experiential Education (cf. Jacoby, 1996). A very large number of higher education institutions in the USA now provide support for community service learning, and increasing numbers of university presidents have committed their institutions to this type of learning through membership of the organization Campus Compact (Ehrlich, 2000; and cf. www.compact.org). What is particularly striking about Higher education in the USA is the extent to which faith-based universities are committed to service learning as part of their theological and faith missions. Today not only is there research being done on pedagogic practices but also, going beyond anecdotal evidence, there is research into the evaluation of the learning outcomes of service learning (cf. Waterman, 1997; Eyler and Giles, 1999; and the special issue of the Michigan Journal of Community Service Learning, Fall 2000). In 2001 the first 'International Service Learning Research Conference' was held at the University of California, Berkeley under the leadership of Dr Andrew Furco and attracted 350 participants.

While there has been a tradition of community-based internship and experiential education since the 1960s, the new emphasis in the USA since the 1990s has been on the link between citizenship education and service learning (Guarasci and Cornwall, 1997; Reeher and Cammarano, 1997; Rimmerman, 1997; Lisman, 1998). This notion of active citizenship not only emphasizes the importance of human rights but also stresses the significance of social responsibility or duty as well as democratic participation. Professor Benjamin Barber, in a number of influential articles and books, has advocated the education for active citizenship in higher education through engaging in critical thinking about politics and civil society and through community service learning. At Rutgers University, Professor Barber has established the Citizenship and Service Education (CASE) programme, which has become an important national model of such an education for citizenship, and more recently at the University of Maryland where he is part of the 'Democracy collaborative'. Recently the Campus Compact under the leadership of Elizabeth Hollander has taken the lead in the USA to promote the civic engagement of higher education and civic engagement across the curriculum (cf. Battistoni, 2002). This is reflected in the growing influence of communitarian politics, especially in the administration of President Bill Clinton and now in the compassionate conservatism of President George W. Bush, Jr. In May 1993, President Bill Clinton outlined proposals for a new type of national service in which one or two years of post-school national service would be paid in the form of a grant towards the cost of education or training, and later in that year the National and Community Service Trust Act (NCSTA) was passed into legislation. At present the Corporation for National Service administers a number of programmes which support service in the community and it also provides backing for research into community service learning in schools (K-12) and higher education (Mohan, 1994). Steve Waldman in his book 'The Bill' analysed the passing of the act and has provided a fascinating case study of the relationship between political values, higher education as big business and the legislative process. President Bush has maintained support for the corporation (which is now called the Corporation for National and Community Service) and its programmes and he has also encouraged links with faith-based community organizations.

Service learning in the UK

In the UK the CSV/Council for Citizenship and Learning in the Community (CSV/CCLC) has been promoting and facilitating education for citizenship and service learning in higher education by working in partnerships with now over 200 programmes in higher education institutions. The aims of this national, multidisciplinary and community-linked network is to promote service learning through university–community partnerships that is accredited or certified and which develops students' skills and citizenship and which meets community needs (Annette, 1999; Annette, Buckingham-Hatfield and Slater-Simmons, 2000). The UK government has established in 2002 the new 'Higher Education Active Community Fund', which has provided funding for the establishment of community service programmes based on effective community partnerships in all English universities but not necessarily establishing service learning programmes. This fund, however, raises the possibility that citizenship education and service learning could become an important feature of higher education in Britain by providing funding for the development of university/community partnerships.

The UK Department for Education and Skills has supported research into work experience (Brennan and Little, 1996; Harvey *et al.*, 1998; Little, 1998), but only recently has it begun to support research into service learning, for example. 'Fund for the Development and Teaching' (FDTL) projects such as the Community Based Learning and Teaching Project, based at the Universities of Birmingham and Liverpool, and the forthcoming research work on the learning outcomes of service learning by Dr David Hall of Liverpool University and Professor John Annette of Middlesex University (Annette, Buckingham-Hatfield and Slater-Simmons, 2000; Hall and Hall, 2002).

Throughout the UK we can find examples of universities recognizing the challenge of establishing partnership working with local and regional communities. Increasingly we can also find evidence of the development of community service and service learning programmes as a response to this challenge. In some higher education systems, however, community partnerships are seen primarily in terms of economic development, cultural formation and technology transfer and not in terms of the curriculum of higher education itself.

It is interesting to note that the UK organization of university and college presidents' report on 'Universities and Communities' (CVCP, 1994), highlighted the role of universities in local and regional development but, except for the appendix by John Mohan, it did not consider how university and community partnerships would impact upon the curriculum of higher education (CVCP, 1994; and for criticisms cf. Watson and Taylor, 1998; Annette, 1999). The main organization of UK university leaders, recently renamed 'Universities, UK', also published in 2002 a series of research-based studies which examined the regional role of higher education institutions but which again largely ignored the role of the curriculum in addressing the needs of regional communities.

Community, communitarianism and higher education

The challenge of introducing the study of citizenship and experiential service learning raises some central questions about the future of higher education and the development of the academic disciplines in the post-Dearing era. With increasing access and public debate about the purpose and accountability of higher education, how will the curriculum in a mass system of higher education address the needs of the academic community and its wider communities? The communitarian agenda in education needs to consider not only the role of schools (Arthur, 2000) but now also higher education. How will generic education for citizenship and community service learning fit into the continuing dominant disciplinary framework? To what extent in the UK will there develop a community-structured problem-based learning that challenges students to think critically about the needs of local communities? To what extent does student-centred learning and the wider use of experiential learning enable students to develop civic and moral values as well as key skills and capabilities and formal academic knowledge, and how will this be reflected in the curriculum of higher education in the future? (cf. Ehrlich *et al.*, 2003). While this may be controversial in the UK context it may be appropriate to consider the role of character education not only in schools but also in higher education (cf. Arthur, 2003 for an excellent introduction to the issue of character education in the UK). This could be based in programmes for student leadership that could be either extra-curriculum-based or integrated into the undergraduate curriculum and which could also involve service learning.

If we are to move beyond sound bites or empty phrases about citizenship and community, it is now central for education both in schools and in higher education to openly debate the issues of education for citizenship and service learning in the community and its place in the curriculum. The challenge for the academic disciplines is about what will be their role in these debates. The challenge for those of us who are establishing service learning and community-based learning programmes will be how we can work in partnership with local communities and the voluntary sector for mutual benefit while providing valuable learning opportunities for citizenship, values and employability for higher education students.

Chapter 5

Searching for a moral North Star during the college years

Arthur Schwartz

Five years ago, my son Tyler organized a football game (American style) on New Year's Eve for 15 of his fifth grade friends (all boys). The game has since turned into an annual event – regardless of rain, snow or freezing temperatures – and my son assures me that the event is now a tradition that will stand the test of time.

This was the first year the boys played as high school students, and as far as I could discern (the game is played across the street from my house in a public park), the lads were enjoying the experience as much as they did when they were in elementary or middle school. As I watched them play, I suddenly realized that these young men, including my son, will be experiencing their 'bright college years' in just four short years.[1]

I have known these boys, and their families, for ten years now, and while I am sure there will be a surprise or two, it is rather easy for me to project how their high school careers will unfold. Overall, these boys are athletically gifted and most of them will play at least one varsity sport. Several of them are academically gifted, and I anticipate that

---

1. The term 'bright college years' is the title of a book by Matthews (1997). The term was a lyric from a nineteenth-century American college song, originating at Yale.

these lads will score very high in the college entrance exams that top-tier US colleges and universities will still be using to select their 2007 freshman class. My sense, however, is that only one or two of the kids (at best) will graduate from high school with any serious vision or commitment to a vocation or professional calling.

Indeed, researchers are beginning to assert that these young men will matriculate to university 'motivated but directionless', to coin the subtitle of *The Ambitious Generation* (Schneider and Stevenson, 1999). Analysing findings from a longitudinal study of school-aged students in the United States, the authors chronicle how a significant number of middle school and high school students are able to recognize that the choices they make today (e.g. whether to work hard and get good grades) will have an impact on their futures tomorrow. To a significant degree, this finding is consonant with an 'achievement orientation' that captures, to a considerable degree, the profile of both my son and his friends.[2]

Against this backdrop of an ambitious and achievement-oriented generation are a growing stack of books and reports published within the past five to ten years lamenting the 'excessive individualism' or 'self-absorption' of the college student as well as her growing civic disengagement and apathy. Interestingly, many of these publications argue that the very structure of an undergraduate education (faculty autonomy, choosing a major, the separation between academic and student life) contributes considerably to what many have come to call the *commodification* of higher education.

A very recent and welcome addition to this literature is *Educating Citizens: Preparing America's Undergraduates for Lives of Moral and Civic Responsibility* (Colby, Ehrlich, Beaumont and Stephens, 2003). Published in collaboration with The Carnegie Foundation for the Advancement

---

2. This orientation to success and achievement was also exquisitely captured by David Brooks in his highly publicized 2001 article in *The Atlantic Monthly* that focused on the students at Princeton University. Brooks writes, '[these students] have woven their way through the temptations of adolescence and have benefited from all the nurturing and instruction and opportunities with which the country has provided them. They are responsible. They are generous. They are bright. They are good-natured. But they live in a country that has lost, in its frenetic seeking after happiness and success, the language of sin and character-building through combat with sin. Evil is seen as something that can cured with better education, or therapy, or Prozac. Instead of virtue we talk about accomplishment.'

of Teaching, and extending the pioneering work of Ernest Boyer, the authors elucidate a series of effective campus-based initiatives (ranging from curricular interventions to out-of-classroom experiences), each designed to shape 'intellectual frameworks' and 'habits of mind' whereby college graduates will see themselves as 'members of a community, as individuals with a responsibility to contribute to their communities' (p. 7). Comparing undergraduate education to an *expedition*, the authors trumpet a set of moral and civic competencies and capacities that they hope will result in shifting a graduate's 'life trajectories just a bit and give them new ways of responding to later experiences' (p. 276). There is, without doubt, much in this book to celebrate and affirm.

Yet I wonder whether the civic values and ideals that animate *Educating Citizens* will enter into the conversations when my son and his friends come home from college in 2007 to play in their annual football game. I suspect not. Indeed, this essay will explore three discreet values that are much more likely to be discussed by my son and his friends before, during, and after their football game. I will argue, moreover, that these values will far more dynamically impact and affect the 'life trajectories' of these young men than the moral and civic values and ideals embedded in the writings of books and publications like *Educating Citizens*.

The first value is *tolerance*. Teaching the language and primacy of tolerance has swiftly become the cardinal virtue of higher education, trumping all other likely suspects (such as intellectual integrity or a concern for truth). Educating for tolerance begins even before a student arrives on campus. At many colleges, students are required during the summer to read a book that stresses one or more areas of diversity (e.g. racial, ethnic, gender, sexual orientation). The themes and perspectives of the book (e.g. oppression, celebration of difference) are usually discussed during a freshman seminar (some of these seminars occur before the academic year begins while others last for the entire first semester). These seminars are the dominant pedagogical site for colleges and universities to *intentionally teach* tolerance as a core value on the college campus. It is during these seminars that students learn about the university's speech code (especially the dangers of ethnic or sex-related jokes!), policies and penalties for sexual harassment, and the university's determination to cultivate an 'inclusive' learning atmosphere. In recent years a significant number of colleges have developed a range of interactive group activities to dramatize various themes, such as asking students to line up by skin color, from lightest to darkest, and asking each one to step forward and talk about how they 'felt' concerning their place in the line.

At the core of these initiatives is the belief and rationale that prejudice is learned and can be unlearned; moreover, that prejudices are attitudes rooted in ignorance and a fear of differences. But while students may become more sensitive to their prejudices, what has resulted is an unanticipated, even onerous consequence: ample evidence is mounting that these multicultural, celebrating diversity programmes have contributed to college students free-falling down the slippery slope of relativism. Because teaching for tolerance rests on the assumption that no value can be held superior to any other value (except for the value of tolerance), colleges and universities are graduating students whose first, foremost, and perhaps only civic loyalty is to the 'Order' of tolerance and diversity. But this loyalty is based less on a celebration of difference than on a grudging and limping indifference. The critic G. K. Chesterton once summed up this condition when he remarked that 'tolerance is a virtue of a man without convictions'. Indeed, there are a growing number of educators who believe the battle cry for this generation can be summed up in the numbing, cynical call of 'Whatever!'

As a society, we are wise to recognize the drastic and significant costs of raising our children with too little tolerance. Moreover, speaking as a Jewish man, I strongly endorse efforts to root out prejudice and bigotry. But there is an equal price to pay if tolerance trumps all other values and virtues we hold dear. We are in danger of educating a generation of students who find such terms as 'convictions' or 'beliefs' as toxic to their well-being. It is safer, both politically and socially, to abstain from holding convictions that may rub someone the wrong way. This widely held perspective is a serious and gnawing problem for college educators striving to create on these campuses an ethos of civic engagement and responsibility.

The second value is *freedom*. Unlike tolerance, which is intentionally taught on our college campuses, freedom is the value most indubitably 'caught'. There are no formal classes in freedom, but right from the very first keg party or late night rap session, college freshman (especially those who do not live at home) are washed in freedom. At its worse, too much freedom becomes a license to behave in ways potentially harmful to the individual and (often) to others. I use the image of the keg party because alcohol use (and misuse) remains the most glaring expression of the 'freedom' that awaits the traditional-aged US college freshman. But there is the day-in and day-out sort of freedom that is just as challenging and difficult to navigate as whether to binge drink at a party or local pub. Of course, college students did not matriculate to university in a moral or ethical straightjacket. But it is within the context of college life where a young person begins to imbibe the reality of individual sovereignty and radical autonomy. Yes, there are courses to pass and other myriad of constraints on one's time and potential choices (e.g. part-time work), but every dean of student life must surely have ready his or her talk to (anxious?) parents that a time-honoured hallmark of an undergraduate education is the opportunity for one's son or daughter to successfully navigate the opportunities (read: temptations) of college life, even if this means, at times, putting her life or health at risk.

It is impossible to understand the nature of freedom on a US college campus without recognizing as well the extent to which our society privileges the value of freedom. The motto of the *Wall Street Journal*, for example, is 'free markets, free people', and clearly the over-whelming majority of US citizens desire to live in a society where economic freedom exists. In our history books, our young read about the struggle for political and religious freedom and soon we come to believe that freedom is a necessary precondition for the pursuit of anyone's individual happiness. Moreover, we purchase each year a plethora of self-help books that reinforce personal self-fulfilment and self-indulgence; one of my favourites is the recent bestseller *Life is Uncertain...Eat Dessert First*. This book underscores the sentiment that freedom is a state-of-mind whereby what we *feel*, as opposed to any other source of authority, is the final arbiter of what is 'true'.

While 'truth' becomes relativized, college adventures in freedom are often ritualized events. Princeton University is famous for its Nude Olympics, the first snow ritual that sends scores of buck-naked sophomores on a midnight run, accompanied by hordes of admirers (the university recently banned the event after ten participants were hospitalized for alcohol poisoning). The University of Virginia is doing its best to stamp out the 'fourth-year fifth', a practice in which seniors drink a fifth of a gallon of alcohol before the final home football game. Hazing practices among some fraternities are also ripe with examples of freedom-gone-amok. Of course, not all of these freedoms revolve around alcohol use: other expressions of 'freedom' emerging on college campuses include gambling on sporting events, promiscuous sex and the joy-of-it shoplifting spree.

In a recent book, Wolfe (2001) argues that the twenty-first century will be known as the century of moral freedom (in contrast to religious, economic or political freedoms that defined previous centuries). Moral freedom, according to Wolfe, means that individuals should determine for themselves what it means to lead a good and virtuous life. Unlike our grandparents, Wolfe suggests that the majority of US citizens faced today with a moral decision look no further than themselves – their own interests, desires, needs, sensibilities, identities and inclinations – before choosing the right course of action.

Within Wolfe's critique, there exists a compelling moral imperative for colleges and universities to explore a variety of approaches to balance, even restrict, a student's freedom (such as regulating frater-nities), a perspective that I recognize represents a significant retreat from the freedoms and rights 'won' by college students in the 1960s and 1970s. How ironic that colleges and universities may be called upon in the twenty-first century to educate its students for lives of *personal responsibility*, against a tsunami wave of freedom and lack of all constraints on behaviour and standards.[3]

The third value is *friendship*. While a number of recent studies have examined the nature and dynamics of one's 'peer culture' on a variety of college-associated behaviours (binge drinking, academic dishonesty, academic achievement, career choices), there exists a paucity of

---

3. What may be at stake is whether colleges and universities can inspire its students, via different pedagogical strategies, to write and live by their own moral constitution. The philosopher Frankfurt (1988) argues for the necessity of moral ideals for the formation of the moral self. He writes: 'A person's ideals are concerns that he cannot bring himself to betray. They entail constraints that, for him, it is unthinkable to violate. Suppose that someone has no ideals at all. In that case, nothing is unthinkable for him; there are no limits to what he might be willing to do. He can make whatever decisions he likes and shape his will just as he pleases. This does not mean that his will is free. It means only that his will is anarchic, moved by mere impulse and inclination. For a person without ideals, there are no volitional laws that he has bound himself to respect and to which he unconditionally submits. He has no volitional boundaries. Thus he is amorphous, with no fixed identity or shape' (24–25).

research on the potency of friendship as a moral educator during the college years. Yet for many of us (including this author), we've experienced the phenomenological truth that it is often within the crucible of friendships that we come to know more about ourselves and the world around us.

Friendship is a moral gift. Friendships teach us how to care for others. Good friends teach us about ourselves, especially those aspects of ourselves we might prefer not to know. Another gift of friendship is that our friends help us stay committed to the most important goals, projects and aspirations of our lives. We also learn about the nature of goodness and virtue through our friends. Finally, a gift of friendship may be the very leverage we need to live more hopefully and truthfully.[4]

Many of us can affirm, from our own personal experience, that these gifts of friendship robustly emerge during the college years. The traditional-aged college freshman may indeed be 'developmentally primed' to invest in such intimate relationships, although I am not aware of any empirically based research to confirm or disconfirm this hypothesis. But it does appear self-evident that during the college years friendships help to shape (for better or worse) our moral lives.

It's relatively straightforward to understand the 'whys' of friendship during the college years. It makes perfect sense for college students flushed in freedom to navigate their freedom with others at their side. While the rhetoric of excessive individualism may be valid as an explanatory construct for a variety of academic and civic outcomes and behaviours, it is rare, to take but one example, for a college student to show up at a keg party alone. It is much more likely that he or she will travel together, not only to parties, but to the myriad of events (such as late night excursions to the local diner) that define so much of the college experience.

I recently had the opportunity to ask dozens of undergraduates about the role of friendship in their lives.[5] As part of their course requirement, I asked each student to (confidentially) describe in writing

---

4. I am indebted to Paul Wadell for my understanding of friendship as both a virtue and a religious ideal. See Wadell (1991, 2002).
5. The course was at the University of Pennsylvania and each undergraduate was a traditional-aged college student.

how their college friendships have already impacted or informed their understanding of ethical behaviour, concern for others or their own personal goals and aspirations. I also invited the students to describe a crucible moment or a specific experience that crystallized for them how friends can help friends become 'the best they can be'. Not a single student had difficulty describing the moral vitality and potency of their friendships. Moreover, I dare say that these narratives of friendship will likely outlast anything 'learned' in the classroom. At least they have in my own life.

Of course, the ideals of friendship must always be tempered against the anvil of extreme. On one side of the coin, colleges and universities should be sensitive to students who have difficulty getting close to anyone, who show a strong reluctance to have or be a friend. On the flip side, historians have amply documented the precarious stroll from a genuine and mutual friendship to a loyalty that is blind and unyielding to other virtues and ends. Within the context of college life, there is growing evidence that one's peer culture has an enormous impact on whether a student lies, steals or cheats related to academic work. That is to say, it is more likely that he or she will learn about an online term paper 'mill' from a friend than from any other source. In sum, the challenge for college officials is to find a way to extend the expression 'friends do not let friends drive drunk' to other domains of campus-based behaviour and ethical standards.

Conclusion

Let me return to my son, his friends and their annual football game on New Year's Eve. The year is 2007 and the boys have just completed their first semester at college. I would not be surprised if, during the game, the boys used language and imagery (sexual-orientation jokes, ethnic slurs) that would get them in considerable trouble if used on the 'quad' or in the hallways of their college dorms. I can even imagine one of the boys ridiculing the regime of 'political correctness' he was subjected to throughout the past semester, regaling his friends about the different ways that his college was coaxing him to recognize his 'privilege' as a white, heterosexual man. It would be far more difficult, I am sure, to discern if the other lads pick up on his anger and resentment – or whether they simply dismiss his rant with a limp 'whatever'.

But once the game is over, and the boys retreat to the basement of our house for some hot chocolate and the latest video games, I would expect the boys, especially those who have not talked to or e-mailed each other since the summer, to begin describing some of the significant experiences they have had since college began. Some may talk about the amazing parties while others would describe in great detail an exciting weekend excursion to the city near where they go to school. I am sure that the topic of girls will surface. And I would not be surprised if one lad (or two) talked about a community service project he has been involved in.

But I suspect that the boys will be most reluctant to talk about their new friendships. They may mention the guys they are hanging out with or playing sports with, but my sense is that these young men will find it very difficult to describe to their high school friends exactly how these new friends are helping them navigate (or not) the storms of freedom we call campus life. What is clear to me, however, from reading the narratives of the students in my class, is that the moral compass college students used during their high school years no longer seems to work as precisely as it once did. For many college students, the undergraduate experience is when they discover and orient themselves to a new moral North Star. And furthermore, it is through the crucible of our friendships whereby we come to see brightly the sort of moral and civic-minded person we want to become. College educators charged with building an ethic of civic responsibility on our campuses would be wise to find ways to dynamically utilize this most powerful taproot of the moral life.

Chapter 6

Citizenship and higher education in the UK

John Annette and Terence McLaughlin

Citizenship and pre-higher education

In recent years citizenship education at pre-higher education level in the United Kingdom has been the focus of much attention by political philosophers, philosophers of education, politicians, policy-makers, educational leaders, teachers and the general public. A major landmark in the extended process of consultation and debate about this matter in England was the report of the Advisory Group on Education for Citizenship and the Teaching of Democracy in Schools chaired by Professor Bernard Crick ('The Crick Report'); (Qualifications and Curriculum Authority, 1998). This report saw citizenship education as comprising three separate but interrelated strands: social and moral responsibility, political literacy and community involvement (for an outline of the essential elements of the report in terms of nine central claims and recommendations see McLaughlin, 2000a: 545–546). The report paved the way for, and shaped the character of, the formal introduction of citizenship education into primary and secondary schools in England from August 2002, supported by a range of requirements and guidelines (on these see, e.g. www.qca.org.uk, www.nc.uk.net, www.dfes.gov.uk/citizenship and www.teachernet.

gov.uk/citizenship). Rather different provisions for citizenship education apply in Wales, Scotland and Northern Ireland (on these see www.wales.gov.uk, www.Scotland.gov.uk and www.deni.gov.uk respectively).

It is worth noting in particular that the Crick report recognized the importance of service learning or active learning in the community, which is based upon the principles of experiential learning (Annette, 2000). Indeed, Bernard Crick holds that what distinguishes political education from citizenship education is community involvement (Crick, 2000b: 115–116). Many schools in the UK now provide school students with the opportunity to engage in the kinds of service learning or 'active learning in the community' which has long been a feature of schools in the USA (see Wade, 1997 for the USA and Annette, 1999 and Potter, 2002 for the UK).

A second Advisory Group on Citizenship, also chaired by Bernard Crick, published a report in 2000 on how the principles and aims of the citizenship order for full-time compulsory schooling (namely, for students up to the age of 16) could be built up to inform the studies of all 16–19 year olds in further education and training (Further Education Funding Council, 2000). This report viewed citizenship as a 'key skill' and argued that all young adults should have an entitlement to citizenship education based on learning through participation rather than learning of a more formal kind and that these students should have the opportunity to have their achievement academically recognized. The report identified skills, roles and knowledge related to citizenship and developed a 'curriculum matrix' to serve as a coherent underpinning to work relating to citizenship, which would be undertaken in many varied learning contexts and in other than prescribed programmes of study (FEFC, 2000, paras 5.6, 5.7, 5.9; Appendix D). A developmental programme of pilot projects began in September 2001, followed by a second programme of pilot projects in 2002 which are being managed by the new Learning and Skills Council Development Agency (see www.citizenshippost-16.LSDA.org.uk). At the time of writing, the Qualifications and Curriculum Authority is drafting guidance to support voluntary, educational, training and work-based providers in developing citizenship programmes and activities for post-16 learners (see www.qca.org.uk). Another aspect of post-16 provision for citizenship is that the Civil Renewal Unit of the Home Office is piloting programmes for adult learning for active citizenship which will be linked to volunteering, community involvement and the activity of becoming a UK citizen.

The ambition of these developments is manifest. The 1998 Report of the Advisory Group on Citizenship insisted that 'We aim at no less than a change in the political culture of this country both nationally and locally: for people to think of themselves as active citizens, willing, able and equipped to have an influence in public life and with the critical capacities to weigh evidence before speaking and acting; to build on and to extend radically to young people the best in existing traditions of community involvement and public service, and to make them individually confident in finding new forms of involvement and action among themselves' (QCA, 1998, para 1.5). The developments are not unproblematic and face many challenges of a wide ranging kind – theoretical as well as practical (for a philosophical assessment of the 1998 Advisory Group report and of citizenship education more generally, see McLaughlin, 2000a. For other assessments and critiques of citizenship education from various perspectives see also, e.g. Beck, 1998, Chs 4, 5; Frazer, 1999a; O'Hear, 1999; Leicester, Modgil and Modgil, 2000; Osler, 2000; Pearce and Hallgarten, 2000; Tooley, 2000; Lockyer, Crick and Annette, 2003).

Regardless of the way in which these developments within the UK may be evaluated in more detailed terms, it can be agreed that they offer a substantial basis for establishing a provision for learning for active citizenship and civil renewal for students up to the age of 19, which is worthy of serious consideration.

What, however, of the role which higher education should play with respect to citizenship? There has been a relative neglect of this matter in the United Kingdom, which perhaps bears out Tomas Englund's observation that, in Western democracies, education for democracy and citizenship has historically been seen as the responsibility of the compulsory school system and as 'not relevant' to higher education (Englund, 2002: 282). The truth or otherwise of this observation depends on precisely how 'education for democracy and citizenship' is being understood. Nevertheless, the role of higher education with respect to citizenship is under-explored and this chapter seeks to bring some central issues relating to this role into clearer focus.

Before proceeding, however, it is illuminating to explore the general underlying social and political perspective which can be argued to underpin the developments concerning citizenship and education which have been outlined.

Civil renewal, new labour and civic republicanism

In the UK the current 'New Labour' government has espoused a pro-gramme of civil renewal that links the public, private and voluntary and community sectors to work for the common good. This is informed by a set of beliefs and values involving faith traditions, ethical socialism, communitarianism and more recently civic repub-licanism. According to the Home Secretary, David Blunkett, 'The "civic republican" tradition of democratic thought has always been an important influence for me...This tradition offers us a substantive account of the importance of community, in which duty and civic virtues play a strong and formative role. As such, it a tradition of thinking which rejects unfettered individualism and criticises the elevation of individual entitlements above the common values needed to sustain worthwhile and purposeful lives. We do not enter life unencumbered by any community commitments, and we cannot live in isolation from others' (Blunkett, 2001: 19). It is this civic republican conception of politics which, we would argue, animates key aspects of New Labour's policies from citizenship education to its strategy towards revitalizing local communities.

One of the key challenges facing civil renewal and the introduction of citizenship education in the UK is the question about whether and in what respects the citizenship is 'British'. Elizabeth Frazer has written about the 'British exceptionalism' towards discussing citizenship (Frazer, 1999a) and David Miller has written that 'citizenship – except in the formal passport-holding sense – is not a widely understood idea in Britain. People do not have a clear idea of what it means to be a citizen. . . . Citizenship is not a concept that has played a central role in our political tradition' (Miller, 2000: 26)

The question concerning to what extent British people are familiar or comfortable with the concept of citizenship raises questions about the extent to which the political language of citizenship and civic republicanism can increasingly be seen as a tradition of 'British' political thought, which can provide the basis for a transformation of the more dominant liberal individualist political traditions (for a recent discussion of matters relating to this, see Ahier, Beck and Moore, 2003, esp. Chs 1, 2). David Marquand in his reassessment of Labour's social democratic politics has written, 'If the argument set out above is right, one obvious if at first sight surprising implication is that the civic republican tradition has more to say to a complex modern society in the late twentieth century than the liberal individualist one; that the protagonists of "active citizenship" are right in laying stress on duty, action, and mutual loyalty, even if wrong in picking certain aspects out of the tradition, while ignoring the rest of the corpus from which they come' (Marquand, 1997: 50–51).

How influential has the civic republican tradition actually been in Britain and to what extent are we witnessing a revival of this political thinking both in contemporary political thought and in the conceptualizing of citizenship as evidenced by the 1998 report of the Advisory Group on Citizenship (Qualifications and Curriculum Authority, 1998) to which reference has already been made? Bernard Crick has acknowledged that the view of citizenship implicit in the report is a civic republican one (Crick, 2000b: 5). Richard Dagger in his influential study of civic education argues that a civic republican conception of citizenship can reconcile both liberal individuality and the cultivation of civic virtue and responsibility. He writes that, 'There is too much of value in the idea of rights – an idea rooted in firm and widespread convictions about human dignity and equality – to forsake it. The task, instead, is to find a way of strengthening the appeal of duty, community and related concepts while preserving the appeal of rights' (Dagger, 1997: 58; and cf. Maynor, 2003).

One of the major challenges facing civic republicanism is that it traditionally identified citizenship with being an educated male property holder. The creation of a shared political identity underlying citizenship should also allow for multiple political identities based on gender, race, ethnicity, social exclusion, etc. It may be that the civic republican politics of contestability, as recently argued for by Philip Pettit (Pettit, 1997), may provide a more pluralist basis for citizenship in contemporary Britain than traditional republican politics. Equally, recent theorists of liberal democracy like Eamonn Callan also argue that an education for citizenship must hold fast to a constitutive ideal of liberal democracy while allowing for religious and cultural pluralism (Callan, 1997). A more differentiated but universal concept of citizenship (Lister, 2003), which encourages civic virtue and participation while maintaining individual liberty and allows for cultural difference, will create a way of understanding citizenship that is appropriate for an education for citizenship and democracy.

It could be argued that for the Prime Minister, Tony Blair, the government's policy of civic renewal is based more on a communitarian concern for a moral and political socialization. Following Elizabeth Frazer's distinction between a 'philosophical communitarianism' and a 'political communitarianism' (Frazer, 1999b), Adrian Little raises some important questions about the apolitical conception of community in communitarianism. He writes that, 'As such, the sphere of community is one of contestation and conflict as much as it is one of agreement. Thus, essentially, it is deeply political. Where orthodox communitarians see politics as something to be overcome to the greatest possible extent, radicals argue that the downward devolution of power will entail more politics rather than less' (Little, 2002: 154). Both Little and Frazer in their studies of the political communitarianism consider the revival of civic republicanism as emerging from the debate between liberal and communitarian conceptions of the politics of community. In civic republicanism (cf. Oldfield, 1990; Petitt, 1997; Maynor, 2003) freedom consists of active self-government and liberty rests not simply on negative liberty but on active participation in a political community.

David Marquand, in his argument for civic republicanism, states that voluntary service is not an important feature of active citizenship. Here I believe he places too much emphasis on formal political participation and the state and does not recognize fully enough the importance of the associations, institutions and practices of civil society. In the USA an increasing number of political scientists, for example, Robert Putnam, are noting the decline of 'social capital' with a decrease in voluntary activity and a growing concern about the vitality of civil society. The evidence in the UK is complex and a recent study indicates that while 'social capital' is still strong there are clear indications of a decline in public 'trust' (Hall, 2002).

A 'strong democrat' like Benjamin Barber argues for the importance of civic engagement and civil society in maintaining a participatory civil society and calls for the maintenance of public spaces for civic participation. According to Barber, 'We live today in Tocqueville's vast new world of contractual associations – both political and economic – in which people interact as private persons linked only by contract and mutual self-interest, a world of diverse groups struggling for separate identities through which they might count for something politically in the national community' (Barber, 1998a). For Barber the fundamental problem facing civil society is the challenge of providing citizens with 'the literacy required to live in a civil society, the competence to participate in democratic communities, the ability to think critically and act deliberately in a pluralist world, the empathy that permits us to hear and thus accommodate others, all involve skills that must be acquired' (Barber, 1992). As we will see later, Benjamin Barber and other political analysts see education for citizenship and service learning in schools and higher education as a key factor in maintaining civic virtue and civic participation. Equally, Robert Wuthnow sees civic participation in civil society as an important way in which people increasingly develop both civic virtues and spiritual moral values and the ability to engage in what the liberal Jewish theorist Michael Lerner has termed the 'politics of meaning' (Wuthnow, 1996, 1997; Lerner, 1997). For civic republicans, however, there is greater emphasis on the devolution of political power and the recognition of the role of civic virtue and participation in local communities. This reflects a gradual shift from reforming to creating new forms of local government to governance and it includes the participation of a range of social networks that can generate both social capital and active citizenship. As Lawrence Pratchett notes, these activities in themselves cannot establish a more deliberative democracy but as part of a wider reform package they can provide the basis for the realization of a deliberative form of democratic politics (Pratchett, 2000).

We shall return in due course to this general underlying social and political perspective which we have been outlining. Now, however, we shall turn to a consideration of initiatives concerning citizenship and higher education which have been developed in the light of, and are broadly consistent with, a perspective of this kind.

Citizenship and higher education

Before proceeding further, it is useful to note that there are a number of different ways in which higher education can contribute to citizenship. This chapter focuses upon the forms of 'education for citizenship' for students which universities may engage in through various forms of influence upon them, including programmes of study and engagement in various activities. In this way, universities make a contribution to the project of 'making citizens' (on the extra-educational factors which contribute to this project see, e.g. Crick, 2001).

However, the contribution of higher education to citizenship is much broader than that to the making of citizens. Universities contribute to the preservation and development of critical traditions of thought which in direct and indirect ways contribute to the resources which enable us to conceptualize the notion of citizenship and bring about its flourishing in any given society in an adequate way. In addition to their role in relation to directly relevant disciplines such as politics, political philosophy and sociology, universities play an indispensable role in support of citizenship by keeping alive the tradition of untrammelled critical enquiry and the maintenance of a kind of protected forum where unpopular, unfashionable and neglected ideas can be systematically explored. More specifically, universities exert a form of 'cultural custodianship' in '…maintaining and continuously revitalizing cultural inheritances' (Graham, 2002: 123) which are significant in a general way for citizenship. Delanty argues that the university has an important role in relation to 'cultural citizenship' and 'technological citizenship', which he sees as importantly related to citizenship in its more familiar social, political and civic senses. With regard to 'cultural citizenship', Delanty outlines a role for the university in the '…critical and hermeneutic…orientation of cultural models…' (Delanty, 2001: 155) as part of the task of giving society a 'cultural direction'. With regard to 'technological citizenship', Delanty sees the university as being in the best position to link the demands of industry, technology and market forces with citizenship as that has been traditionally understood (see also Delanty, 2000). Universities therefore contribute in both a direct and indirect way to the stock of social, political and cultural ideas and ideals prevalent in a society at any particular time, many of which are not only significant for citizenship but required by it. Sir Stewart Sutherland argues that the major contribution of the university to civic virtue is the spread of sense and practical wisdom in society (reported in Blake, Smith and Standish, 1998: 101). (On the responsibilities of the academic profession to society, see Shils, 1997: 89–118 and on the relationship between the modern university and liberal democracy see Shils, 1997: 250–290.)

Another dimension of the contribution of higher education to citizenship comes into focus in the observation of Barnett and Standish that, 'One does not get far in contemporary discussions of the university before one is caught up in complex questions of social justice' (Barnett and Standish, 2003: 215). Issues of access to, and funding of, higher education are highly sensitive for citizenship, not least through their relationship with equality of opportunity: such issues can therefore rightly be seen as part of the 'citizenship agenda' for higher education (on the implications for citizenship of the restructuring of higher education in the UK see Ahier, Beck and Moore, 2003, Ch. 3).

Universities also make a contribution to citizenship through their work in the education and training of professionals whose responsibilities are citizenship-sensitive, most notably teachers. In addition, it should be remembered that universities are also large 'corporate actors' within their own local communities and this generates expectations and duties with respect to good 'citizenship behaviour' (e.g. in relation to appropriate employment practices and the promotion of ecologically appropriate policies).

In the concept of the 'service university' the role of higher education with respect to citizenship and its local community is seen in direct terms. It is important, therefore, to see the role of higher education in relation to citizenship as broader than that of 'making citizens'. The role of 'making citizens' is, however, the primary concern of this chapter.

Higher education institutions in the USA have been engaged more extensively and explicitly in the preparation of its students to be citizens than their counterparts in the UK. Harry Boyte has invoked the tradition of 'public work', which he argues goes beyond both liberal individualism and communitarianism, and he has applied it to the movement for educational reform in higher education in the USA. According to Boyte and Kari, 'Recasting civic education as the public work of higher education holds potential to move the collective efforts in civic renewal to a new stage. But this will entail re-examination of traditional pedagogy, scholarship, the public traditions of disciplines and systems of reward, among other things. As public cultures are recreated within institutions, the culture itself becomes a kind of overall pedagogy for such work' (Boyte and Kari, 2000: 51).

In the 1999 in the USA, the national organization, Campus Compact, established the 'Presidents Declaration on the Civic Responsibility of Higher Education', which was written by Thomas Ehrlich of the Carnegie Foundation for the Advancement of Teaching and Elizabeth Hollander, executive director of the Campus Compact. It was drafted with the assistance of a distinguished 'President's Leadership Colloquium', which included Derek Bok, the president emeritus of Harvard University. As of 2004 some 528 presidents of universities and colleges of higher education in the USA have signed the declaration. This document was itself influenced by the 'Wingspread Declaration on Renewing the Civic Mission of the American Research University', which was written by Harry Boyte of the University of Minnesota and Elizabeth Hollander of Campus Compact (cf. Ehrlich, 2000 and www.compact.org). In 2003 the 'Association of American Colleges and Universities' and Campus Compact established the 'Center for Liberal Education and Civic Engagement' which is engaged in doing research into the civic-engaged curriculum.

There is a long tradition of linking civic engagement and higher education in the USA from Thomas Jefferson's University of Virginia to the Land Grant universities of the nineteenth century. Educational thinkers have also made this link from the democratic education ideas of John Dewey to the idea of the engaged campus of Ernest Boyer and to the more recent concerns with the civic responsibility of higher education given the decline of social capital according to Robert Putnam (cf. Ehrlich, 2000). Intellectually, the ideas of the American pragmatists and especially John Dewey have been an important influence on developing this linkage between citizenship and higher education through experiential learning (Harkavy and Benson, 1998; and cf. Ryan, 1997). What is particularly important about this pragmatic tradition of thought is how it has encouraged academics in higher education to periodically rethink the 'liberal education' curriculum and to consider how through forms of active, problem-based, and service learning it can encourage the moral and civic education of undergraduates (Kimball, 1995; Orrill, 1995, 1998; Benson and Harkavy, 2002).

Unlike the USA, most of the mission statements of universities and colleges of higher education in the UK do not use the rhetoric of civic republicanism and do not talk about promoting citizenship or civic responsibility. 'Universities, UK', the main organizations of university heads, has published a study of 'Universities and Communities' (CVCP, 1994) and more recently has commissioned research into the regional roles of higher education institutions (Universities, UK, 2001). There is no discussion in these documents of the wider civic role of universities and colleges and there are certainly no proposals to consider how the undergraduate curriculum might enable students to develop their moral and civic capacity for active citizenship. This is also true of the recent government 'White Paper' on 'The Future of Higher Education', which concentrated much more on the funding mechanisms for higher education and on the need for more technology and business partnerships (cf. Collini, 2003).

While there are only a few researchers in the UK who are currently attempting to argue for the civic role of higher education (e.g. Coffield and Williamson, 1997; Mohan, 1997; Annette, 1999; Annette Buckingham-Hatfield and Slater-Simmons, 2000; Hall, 2002; Ahier, Beck and Moore, 2003), there is in fact an interesting history in the UK of linking civic engagement and higher education, which has been largely ignored in the present discussions of the purpose and future of higher education. For example, the Scottish Universities, as part of the legacy of the Scottish Enlightenment, were influenced by civic ideals and the study of moral philosophy, which became an integral part of the undergraduate curriculum (Davie, 1961; Winch, 1978). This civic idealism continued to be important in Scotland in the late nineteenth century and influenced the establishment of the 'civic universities' in the nineteenth century by reforming dissenting elites in the new industrial cities of England. In many respects these traditions of civic higher education continued until the emergence of academic disciplines and the establishment of the dominant model of the research university in the twentieth century. Another important intellectual tradition, which is to a large extent forgotten by educationalists today, is that of British idealism. T. H. Green, for example, not only considered education as a means of self-realization but also saw learning as an integral part of a democratic participatory society.

It was also T. H. Green, a key influence on the development of British Idealism at Oxford, who was influential in the establishment of Toynbee Hall in the East End of London and the University Settlement Movement. His influence inspired idealistic young undergraduates to go to the inner cities to serve the poor as part of their ethical and civic duty (Boucher and Vincent, 2000: 27–29).

To a certain extent the ideas of the British Idealists influenced the New Liberalism of the early twentieth century and the higher educational reform ideas of R. B. Haldane, H. L. Fisher and A. D. Lindsay, who founded Keele University. These ideas also influenced the 'Robbins Report' of 1963, which called for the expansion of higher education while maintaining a commitment to the civic purpose of higher education, which is largely missing in the Dearing commission Report of 1997. While the development of the research university was slower in the UK than that in the USA, by the late 1960s the earlier liberal ideas of education had largely disappeared from British higher education. It had given way to the disciplinary framework of the research university which still exists today and which is different from the still influential liberal arts framework in the undergraduate curriculum in the USA. The recent government 'White Paper' on 'The Future of Higher Education' while addressing both the globalization of higher education and the need for more support for innovation in teaching and learning also fails to address the issue of the civic role of universities and colleges of higher education in the UK. Despite the lack of a major movement for developing the civic role of higher education in the UK, there are an increasing number of academics who are now arguing for higher education to participate more fully in civil renewal. According to Crick, 'Universities are part of society and, in both senses of the word, a critical part which should be playing a major role in the wider objectives of creating a citizenship culture. I am now far from alone in arguing this' (Crick, 2000b: 145).

Higher education, citizenship, civic responsibility and service learning

As indicated in an earlier chapter in this book there are in higher education in the UK an increasing number of academic programmes which provide learning for active citizenship through what has been called either active learning in the community, community-based learning or service learning (Annette, 1999, 2003b; and cf. Astin, 2002). This has influenced the Dearing Commission into Higher Education (1997), which called for a greater emphasis in the undergraduate curriculum on the development of key skills and work-related or community-based learning. This pedagogy of experiential learning is based on the learning cycle of David Kolb and has now firmly established itself in higher education and professional development. As a form of learning it is based not just on experience but on a structured learning experience with measurable learning outcomes. A key element of this type of learning is that it is based on reflection by the student on their activity of volunteering or civic engagement. This has been assisted by the Higher Education Active Community Fund (HEACF), which is an HEFCE fund that is assisting universities and colleges of higher education in England to promote volunteering and community partnerships. While this has resulted in the certification of volunteering or community service, there have been an increasing number of academic programmes which accredit the learning involved. There is the CSV/Council for Citizenship and Learning in the Community (CCLC), which is a national network of community-based learning or service learning programmes which holds a national conference and is now linked to over two hundred programmes in UK higher education institutions. Increasingly these programmes in the UK promote learning not just for generic life skills but also for the knowledge, skills and understanding necessary for active citizenship. Professor Benjamin Barber, in a number of influential articles and books, has advocated the education for active citizenship through engaging in critical thinking about politics and civil society and through service learning. While there has been a tradition of community-based internship and experiential education since the 1960s, the new emphasis in the USA since the 1990s has been on the link between citizenship education and service learning (Guarasci and Cornwall, 1997; Reeher and Cammarano, 1997; Rimmerman, 1997). There is also an increasing emphasis on the need for service learning programmes to meet the needs of local community partners (Cruz and Giles, 2000; Gelmon *et al.*, 2001). Service learning can not only help build a type of 'bridging as well as bonding social capital' (cf. Putnam, 2000), it may also develop the capacity building for democratic citizenship within civil society (Annette, 1999; Kahne *et al.*, 2000; Battistoni, 2002). An important research question which needs to be examined is, what are the necessary elements of a service learning programme which can build not only social capital but also active citizenship (Campbell, 2000; Kahne *et al.*, 2000; Annette, 2003b).

In the USA Thomas Ehrlich and Anne Colby and associates have recently published the initial findings of the project of the Carnegie Foundation for the Advancement of Teaching on 'Higher Education and the Development of Moral and Civic Capacity' (Ehrlich *et al.*, 2003; and cf. www.kml.carnegiefoundation.org/mcr/). They argue that, 'Moral and civic development has always been central to the goals of liberal education. In fact, we believe that the movement to strengthen undergraduate moral and civic education is best understood as an important part of the broader efforts to revitalise liberal education, which many commentators have suggested has lost its way in the era since World War II' (Ehrlich *et al.*, 2003: 23; and cf. Orrill, 1995, 1998). In their study they examine the programmes and campus cultures of twelve diverse higher education institutions in the USA. As they clearly recognize, only a limited number of universities and colleges in the USA provide a full range of learning opportunities for active citizenship despite the increasing influence of the pedagogy of service learning. These institutions approach the learning of civic and moral responsibility in different ways which can include the building of the student's character or virtues, both moral and civic, an emphasis on social responsibility or social justice and also engagement with local communities. These ways are linked to a variety of pedagogical approaches from student leadership education, active and problem-based learning, to issues-based democratic deliberative forums, to service learning, etc., which have been developed in most of the 12 higher education institutions who are participating in this project. In the UK there are now a number of pilot student leadership programmes (e.g. The York Awards, the Exeter University student leadership programme and the Middlesex University 'Leadership and Citizenship Award Programme') but we do not fully enough link this with character education (cf. Arthur,

2003). In addition, there are a variety of experiential and active learning pedagogies being introduced in UK higher education but nothing like the Kettering Foundation 'National Issues Forums' in the USA which promote the knowledge and skills of deliberative democracy. While the Teacher Training Agency in the UK has provided school teachers with a number of initiatives to support them, there has been no equivalent resource that has been provided for academics in higher education.

What is particularly interesting about the study by Colby and Ehrlich for the Carnegie Foundation for the Advancement of Teaching is its insistence that learning through 'political engagement' is necessary for providing a full education for citizenship in higher education as distinct from the wider experience of civic engagement. They write that, 'Even in this relatively broad definition of political engagement, not all forms of civic involvement counts as political' (Ehrlich *et al.*, 2003: 19). Thus service learning that is based on solely on volunteering and does not address public policy issues is not seen as providing the type of experiential learning through political engagement that they consider necessary for an education for citizenship. There is, therefore, a need to conceptualize what is the 'political' in examining how an education for citizenship might be introduced into the curriculum of higher education in the UK (cf. Crick, 2000a for a consideration of what constitutes the political and its importance for democracy). According to Bernard Crick, 'Some leading politicians in both countries try to bridge the contradiction between the convenience of liberal democratic theory for the conduct of government and the more disruptive, unpredictable civic republican theory. They try to reduce, whether sincerely or cynically, citizenship to "volunteering" or in the USA, "service learning"' (Crick, 2002).

One of the challenges in providing experiential learning, which involves forms of political engagement, is the evidence that increasingly young people are still interested in involvement in their communities but are alienated from the formal political process (cf. Hall, 2002; Annette, 2003b). Colby and Ehrlich argue that we need to analyse the motivations that encourage students to take advantage of these learning opportunities for active citizenship. In the UK in a recent qualitative study, students at Anglia Polytechnic University and Cambridge

University were analysed to consider how they learn both formally and informally for citizenship to become what are called 'graduate citizens' (Ahier, Beck and Moore, 2003). While this study has, I believe, a somewhat limited understanding of contemporary citizenship and community, its lifecourse research reinforces the contradiction between students who want to become involved in their communities but are turned off from politics. (On the differing ways in which 'civic participation' can be understood see, e.g. Preston, 2004.) It also raises the issue that students are aware of the effects of globalization on themselves and their local communities and that an education for citizenship in higher education must take into account the role of global civil society (Delanty, 2000; Dower, 2003; Annette, 2003b). The research of Colby and Ehrlich also argue that, following Youniss and Yates (1997) and Verba, Schlozman and Brady (1995), the development of an identity as an active citizen within students in higher education is similar to the development of moral behaviour as analysed by Kohlberg and by theorists of character development. Much more research is needed into the moral development of higher education students to better understand how a curriculum for active citizenship might be best developed in the UK.

Finally, it should be noted that one area in UK higher education where there is an increasing interest in learning for active citizenship is in Faculties of Continuing Education. This is important given the fact that increasingly students in higher education study part-time and are mature students (Watson and Taylor, 1998; Coare and Johnston, 2003). According to Chris Duke, 'What needs to happen to empower the student to feel part and to be an active part of his or her society? What need you learn and must you be able to do – and feel – to contribute to societal learning? What are the skills of civic and political participation, and where do they appear in the curriculum of higher education? It will be necessary to keep asking these questions to sustain a relevant and effective lifelong learning curriculum' (Duke, 1997: 69). What is needed to develop a lifelong learning continuum for active citizenship in the UK is to share knowledge, professional practice and research findings across the boundaries of schools, the 16–19 curriculum, further education (pre-degree community colleges), higher education and higher-education-based continuing education.

Citizenship, higher education and the 'making of citizens' in critical perspective

The initiatives and developments that have been outlined above relating to the role of citizenship and higher education in the 'making of citizens' require further exploration and defence in the light of the consideration of a number of critical questions.

It is important to note that many aspects of the influence of the university on students are significant for the 'making of citizens'. In terms of the formal curriculum of the university, the study of any serious subject can, in virtue (say) of the development of the sorts of general critical understanding and sensibility described earlier, contribute to citizenship. Gordon Graham argues that, '...criticism of social policies and political parties will inevitably arise in a context where there is a more general commitment to the pursuit of truth and to freedom of enquiry' (Graham, 2002: 123). It will also be recalled that cultural and technological, as well as social and political, understanding and 'literacy' can contribute to citizenship understood in broad terms. The experience of students in the life and work of the university as a whole, including its relationships, procedures and 'ethos' are also rich in its implication for citizenship.

This general point gives rise to a query about the extent to which universities should be directly concerned with the 'making of citizens' as distinct from seeing such 'making' as an indirect consequence of the study, life and work of the university conceived in broader terms. Gordon Graham distinguishes between the *benefit* gained by engaging in an activity and the *point* of doing so. Thus, whilst physical fitness is not the *point* of playing football, it may nevertheless be a *benefit* of playing (Graham, 2002: 42). Thus conceptions of higher education which lay an emphasis upon (say) the development of knowledge and study for its own sake and upon an associated general enrichment of the mind and understanding may be argued to be contributing to education for citizenship in a broad sense. Many of the wider benefits of learning (on these see Schuller *et al.*, 2004) have resonances for the experience and exercise of aspects of citizenship. These include the development of attitudes such as tolerance (op. cit.: 124–136) and the encouragement of forms of civic association and participation which are not confined to the strictly political (Preston, 2004) nor, it might be argued, require the engagement in forms of study and activity framed directly in terms of 'education for citizenship'. (For a discussion of the significance of general forms of study for citizenship in the context of the school, see Pring, 1999. On the communal goods of academic subjects, see Blake, Smith and Standish, 1998, Ch. 2.)

This line of argument is significant because the extent to which higher education might be argued to have a role of a direct kind in the 'making of citizens' is, for various reasons, contested. It is therefore important to note that such 'making' is nevertheless taking place in some form however the role of the university is conceived.

One ground on which it may be denied that the university has a direct role in the 'making of citizens' is that such a role is not a part of the aims, values and purposes of higher education, properly understood. The aims, values and purposes of higher education are, of course, notoriously contested and controversial. Gordon Graham cautions that a 'purism' about these aims, values and purposes is not only out of place but has in fact never been in place. Graham argues, for example, that a concern with knowledge and the pursuit of learning for their own sake rather than for some external practical end have always co-existed in universities, including ancient universities, with a concern to provide forms of practical training (Graham, 2002: 19–21; see also Ch. 1).

However, whilst it is appropriate to be cautious in referring in an unguarded way to the 'traditional' concept of the university, it is nevertheless possible to identify a cluster of elements in well-established but currently embattled conceptions of the university which are in tension with the claim that it should have a direct role in the 'making of citizens'. A prominent element here is the claim that the university is, '...first and foremost a haven within which the free pursuit of rational inquiry, wherever it may lead, is made secure...' (Graham, 2002: 125). The university is not *for* something. As Oakeshott puts it: 'A university is not a machine for achieving a particular purpose or producing a particular result; it is a manner of human activity' (Fuller, 1989: 96). A further prominent element in such conceptions is a distance from contemporary life and its demands as seen in Oakeshott's conception of a university as offering to students 'the gift of an interval' (Fuller, 1989: 127). Other elements include an emphasis on non-instrumentality in what is to be taught and learnt, sensitivity to the distinction between education and training, an emphasis on the achievement of personally transformative deep and connected understanding rather than on skills or competences, and so forth. A particular perspective on the inappropriateness of the university as a context for the direct 'making of citizens' can be seen in Oakeshott's characterization of the nature of political education (Fuller, 1989: 136–158). (On elements of conceptions of the university of the sort indicated here in contrast to recent developments in higher education see, e.g. Fuller, 1989; Blake, Smith and Standish, 1998; Graham, 2002; Maskell and Robinson, 2002.) The power of such conceptions of the university is manifest, despite the various critiques and pressures which they have been subject to (on such critiques and pressures see, e.g. Barnett, 1990; Delanty, 2001; Barnett and Standish, 2003; Stevens, 2004).

The perception that the university should attempt to 'make citizens' in a more direct way is, however, widely felt, as indicated above. The 'indirect citizenship effects' of a university education are widely felt to be insufficient or in some cases harmful, for example, where the citizenship-sensitive demands of identity and recognition are inadequately attended to (Ahier, Beck and Moore, 2003: 44–48).

It is important to note that resources exist within the kinds of conceptions of the university which we have been discussing for a more direct role to be taken with respect to the 'making of citizens'. The ideal of 'liberal education' which is implicit in these conceptions of the university is, after all, strongly sensitive to citizenship in that the sort of 'freedom' which the ideal embodies has social and political dimensions and imperatives. Blake, Smith and Standish argue that the 'empowerment' with which higher education is concerned should include 'a robust conception of citizenship', where '...students take on the role of contributing to the development and shaping of their society in ways that are in part expressive of themselves but through which they in some sense find themselves' (Blake, Smith and Standish, 1998: 48). Nussbaum in her book 'Cultivating Humanity: A Classic Defense of Reform in Higher Education' (Nussbaum, 1997, see also 2002) has argued that the kinds of conceptions of the university outlined above need to be extended and modified in order to achieve a liberal educational ideal of this kind more adequately in the circumstances of contemporary life. More specifically she argues that universities should consider introducing curriculum reform, including a segment of general 'education for citizenship' for all students (2002: 293), in order to achieve three capacities which are seen as necessary if not sufficient for 'the cultivation of humanity in today's interlocking world' (ibid.: 293): the capacity for critical examination of oneself and one's traditions as part of the living of 'the examined life' and realization of the norm of deliberative democracy, the development of the capacity of students to see themselves as citizens not merely of a local region but as tied together with all human beings by ties of 'recognition' and 'concern', and the development of the critical narrative imagination as part of the ability to put oneself in the shoes of other people (1997, Chs 1–3). Nussbaum sees the curriculum implications of these aims in wide ranging terms, and as requiring a mixture of basic required courses which all students must take (including 'Socratic philosophising' and a confrontation with carefully chosen literary works to awaken the narrative imagination) and the infusion of world-citizenship perspectives in advanced courses in the different disciplines. Nussbaum can therefore be seen as extending the agenda for universities more in the direction of a form of direct 'making of citizens' even if her conception of citizenship is broader than that employed in our discussion above, and if specifically political forms of understanding are from some points of view underemphasized. (For complexities and difficulties in the notion of a liberal conception of higher education in general, see Barnett, 1990; Delanty, 2001; Barnett and Standish, 2003.)

It may be felt that a proposal such as Nussbaum's, whilst softening the 'ivory tower' character of the traditional conception of the university, is still not direct and practical enough as an approach to the 'making of citizens'. It is in this context that the demands for the sort of service learning which has been indicated above come into focus, together with an invitation to a related adjustment of the conception of the role of the university. Two points about such learning as a form of direct 'making of citizens' can usefully be made, in relation to which dangers for service learning can be identified. First, it is an important feature of any worthwhile conception of higher education that it seek the development of a certain kind of rich and connected understanding. (For an outline of the features which should characterize a subject apt for study at degree level see Blake, Smith and Standish, 1998: 44–45.

On the nature of a form of 'rational deliberation' which universities should seek to promote, and which is relevant to citizenship, see Blake, Smith and Standish, 1998: 63–64.) One danger confronting forms of service learning is that they will fail to embody and develop the sorts of understanding and rational deliberation which are required for an adequately conceived form of citizenship. This danger is related to the second point and its danger. Citizenship, both as a concept and in terms in which it may be actualized and institutionalized in any specific context, is inherently contested. This includes 'active citizenship' and the kind of social and political perspective underlying it, which was outlined earlier (on this see, e.g. McLaughlin, 2000a: 549–554). The danger therefore is that if service learning inadequately embodies and develops appropriate forms of understanding and deliberation, students will be encouraged unreflectively into forms of activity which are underjustified. (On similar dangers with respect to the promotion by higher education of a form of European Citizenship, see McLaughlin, 2000b.) In this matter, much hangs on the extent to which the reflective aspects of service learning require the synoptic and wide ranging critical resources of the kind embedded in Nussbaum's proposal.

It should be noted, however, that in relation to the role of the university in the 'making of citizens' both a proposal such as Nussbaum's and proposals relating to the development of forms of service learning confront a specific challenge relating to the current nature of higher education in general. This challenge is brought into focus by Alasdair MacIntyre's lament in relation to the specialization and compartmentalization characteristic of contemporary universities, which have become in his view, '...mere assemblages of assorted disciplinary enterprises' (MacIntyre, 2001: 2) and '...a set of assorted and heterogenous specialized enquiries into a set of assorted and heterogenous subject matters...' (ibid.: 5). For MacIntyre, whilst research and instruction in specialized academic disciplines have an essential place in universities, it is a secondary one: such activities have a 'due place' in universities only insofar as they serve a 'further end' '...that of contributing to and finding their place within an integrated understanding of the order of things' (ibid.: 1). In MacIntyre's view, the neglected 'integrative' tasks of universities have an important role in bringing about the development and exercise of a full range of the powers of understanding and judgement of students in a form of self-transformation involving the achievement of 'completed understanding' and wisdom. MacIntyre sees the 'integrative tasks' of universities as central to the ideal of liberal education, and to its aspiration to liberate the minds of students from, '...preconceptions imposed upon them by the established culture' (ibid.: 13). Students must be helped to see their lives as a whole and to combat a contemporary tendency to lead compartmentalized lives. MacIntyre's own account of the 'integrative tasks' of universities is drawn from the context of Catholic thought and its theologically informed vision of the human person and the human world. Any direct role on the part of universities in the 'making of citizens' seems, however, to imply and require the identification and achievement of a form of holistic and integrated perspective on this matter. In the absence of this it is difficult to see how core curricula can be identified, specified and enacted (as in proposals such as those of Nussbaum) and appropriate forms of service learning incorporated in a systematic way in the programme and life of the university. Much of value in the 'making of citizens' by universities can doubtless be achieved by piecemeal initiative and innovation. If, however, this aspect of the work of universities is to be recognized and is to take root in a deeper way, attention is needed to the challenge arising from one of the most salient features of the modern university: its specialized and compartmentalized nature.

Chapter 7

Character education at the university: a worthy purpose[1]

Karen E. Bohlin

> Many people have a wrong idea of what constitutes real happiness. It is not obtained through self-gratification but through fidelity to a worthy purpose.
>
> Helen Keller

As Helen Keller eloquently stated, true happiness stems from our 'fidelity', our capacity to identify and invest ourselves in 'a worthy purpose'. In my own experience as a professor, I have found that many students – even those who seem externally successful – are disillusioned precisely because they lack this sense of purpose, as well as the guidance or habits of reflection that would facilitate their search for worthy goals. Chuck Eesley, a recent graduate from Duke University, describes the crisis of meaning that so many university students are facing: 'The thing that concerns me most is the amount of apathy and disillusionment I see around me....People get such tunnel vision from...their busy, hectic lives of adding to a resume, racking up accomplishments, getting ahead, that no one has time to really step back and try to see the forest instead of just the trees.'

---

1. This chapter builds on ideas explored in an article I wrote for the special issue of the *Journal of Education* (2000), 'Can virtue be taught at the university?' Vol. 182.

To be able to develop this larger vision and to live in accordance with it, virtue – both moral and intellectual – is essential. Virtue has much to do with happiness because, as Aristotle observes, living virtuously – far from following a rigid code or arbitrary set of values – is directly related to happiness, *eudaimonia* or human flourishing. Virtue provides an internal compass, a wisdom that enables one to discover worthwhile goals, and a set of dispositions – self-mastery, courage, justice – that facilitate the pursuit of these goals.

As a university education so often corresponds with the time young adults chart their course for the future, attention to virtue is essential. Universities and professors cannot be indifferent with regard to the character of their students if they want them to flourish as human beings and to make a positive contribution to their society. Besides, engaging in some type of character education is inevitable. The President of Wake Forest University, Thomas Kearn, argues the following:

> Despite the academic orthodoxies of the moment, in fact there is no education or educational process that does not invoke a regulative ideal of the truth. Whatever we may say, education aims to remove barriers that prevent students from seeing and understanding things as they are; that is, to see the world truthfully.... Education is, as Aristotle said, a moral process. So we are always doing character education. The only issue is whether these initiatives are purposeful or thoughtless.

In this chapter, I would like to present some reflections on the nature of character education, its particular importance in university education today, and the ways in which professors can have a positive influence on the character of their students. I hope that these reflections may help to inspire a more conscious and purposeful approach to character education at the university level.

Character education: choice, vision and desire

Because virtue consists not primarily in theoretical knowledge but in good judgement and right action, the most powerful education in virtue comes not from a lesson or an abstract ideal, but from a life.

We know from experience that conceptions of the good life vary greatly not only from one individual to another but also from one stage of a person's life to another. Since antiquity it has been commonplace for wise persons to observe that popular notions of the good life as devoted to the accumulation of wealth, honours and power or as given over to the pursuit of pleasure are misguided.[2] Human beings are more likely to flourish if they attend to those internal characteristics that define who they are themselves, rather than focusing on life's external trappings of success.

When we recall, for example, Anne Frank's hope and compassion while hiding in Nazi-occupied Amsterdam and Anne Sullivan's doggedness in teaching Helen Keller; when we reflect on Gandhi's and Martin Luther King's commitment to justice at the risk of losing their lives; when we witness Nelson Mandela's and Nien Cheng's continuing personal battles against political oppression, we come to understand virtue in its most admirable incarnations. While these individuals faced dramatically different challenges, they share a common denominator: 'fidelity to a worthy purpose'.

While their accomplishments may seem too extraordinary to achieve, their strength of character and breadth of vision are within reach, if they are developed as a result of smaller choices made on daily basis, choices made in keeping with noble goals. These exemplary lives highlight the fact that, whatever the circumstances, human beings are free to choose how they will respond. A virtuous person is one who knows how to choose well in the variety of complex situations that life presents.

The film version of Anne Frank (Touchstone, 2001) based on Mueller's Biography of Anne Frank brings this to light. In the 'Secret Annexe' we witness each individual's choice of response to the same adverse circumstances. Mr Frank's motto, 'Hope and work', lived daily, stands in stark contrast to Mr Van Pelt's restless pursuit of food and cigarettes – especially as he puts the safety of others at risk.

Viktor Frankl (1984), concentration camp survivor and renowned psychiatrist, underscores the connection between choice and character in his *Man's Search for Meaning*:

---

2. cf. Aristotle, *Nicomachean Ethics*, Book 1.

We who lived in the concentration camps remember the men who walked through the huts comforting others, giving away their last piece of bread. They may have been few in number, but they offer sufficient proof that everything can be taken from a man but one thing: the last of the human freedoms – to choose one's attitude in any given set of circumstances, to choose one's own way. . . .

Even though conditions such as lack of sleep, insufficient food and various mental stresses may suggest that the inmates were bound to react in certain ways, in the final analysis it became clear that the sort of person the prisoner became was the result of an inner decision, and not the result of camp influences alone. (p. 75)

Whereas the challenges students face at the university do not approach the horrors endured by Frankl and others, students are met with their own tests of character. Stephen Tigner divides these tests into two broad categories: the stress tests of character and the leisure tests of character.[3] The stress tests involve external challenges to character. These challenges are usually related to some type of fear – fear of pain and suffering, fear of what other people will think, fear of failure, fear of losing something we deem essential to our happiness, fear of the unknown – and are surmounted with courage or fortitude. The leisure tests of character come primarily from internal temptations – immoderate desires for pleasure, comfort, food, entertainment, etc. – that require self-mastery to overcome.

The stress tests that students face are many. Some arrive at a new and unfamiliar campus on the heels of their parents' recent divorce or a death in the family. Faced with the burden of having to support themselves, they are overwhelmed from the start. Some students battle depression, others contend with eating disorders, addiction or sexual abuse. Some students experience life-altering injuries through sports or an accident. The list goes on. We meet these students each year. Some are at the point of drowning and others gracefully navigating their stormy seas.

Stress tests of character can also be less dramatic. All students face the pressure to perform well in academic classes, sports, clubs and

---

3. Steven S. Tigner first describes the stress test and the leisure test of character in his article 'Signs of the soul', in G. S. Fain (ed.), *Leisure and Ethics: Reflections on the Philosophy of Leisure* (Volume II). Reston VA: American Association for Leisure and Recreation, 1995, 9–24.

even social life. Fear of losing a scholarship, or of not living up to parental expectations, may push a student to consider cheating on an exam or a paper. Social competition may lead some students to be disloyal to friends in order to ingratiate themselves with a new, more popular crowd, or to win acceptance into the most selective fraternity. Kevin Krauth, a student at Duke University writing for a seminar that focused on ethics in college life, explains some of the stresses that he and his peers face.

> In an environment so overwrought with achievement and excellence, people are afraid of being blown away by the competition and, as a result, the option to cheat or illicitly acquire advantages over others looms ominously over our heads. People regularly bend and even break their moral or ethical code in the name of competition.

The choices that students make in response to these 'stress tests' reveal much about their character, and also – because virtue is formed by habit – set the stage for the choices they will make in the future, when faced with ethical dilemmas in their workplace or family.

Ordinary life, and the new-found freedom that college provides, also presents daily challenges to students' character. Who we are is equally disclosed by the choices we make when we have the leisure to do whatever we want. What do students choose when faced with the leisure test of character – when they are living on their own with many tantalizing options and few external boundaries – free to spend their time and money as they please?

There is nothing new about this simple truth: from Aristotle to Anne Frank, it is evident that who we are, our character, is revealed by what we choose. The ability to choose well in the face of stress or leisure stems in large part from the ability to see the various objects of our choice for what they are, to have that internal compass that virtue provides. What does it mean to see well? The discriminating mind is able to assess a situation, to see beyond the immediate or superficial appearances of things. The discriminating mind can make distinctions, for example, between impulse and intelligent choice, between friendship and exploitation, between healthy self-respect and self-aggrandizement, between treating others as colleagues and treating them as stepping-stones.

When we are led by blind ambition, emotion or passion, we retain the freedom to choose, but we lose our capacity to choose well. Our judgement is blurred. We deceive ourselves (willingly or unwittingly) into believing that we have chosen well when we have simply rationalized a bad decision. Lust for power, for example, drove Macbeth to kill King Duncan. After assuming the throne, however, his ambitions are quickly laid waste by guilt and misery. Sentimentality can also hinder our capacity to see. Blind *eros* drove Gatsby to build an empire in order to woo Daisy back, and yet his romantic dream ended in a tragic nightmare. In short, when our vision is misdirected, the capacity to invest ourselves in 'a worthy purpose' is thwarted.

Whether for good or for ill, our vision is directed by desire. The outcome depends on the quality of our desires. Desires can be base or noble, useful or pleasant, as Aristotle points out. Discerning the merit of one's desire and harmonizing conflicting desires are essential to intellectual and moral maturity. Since desire ultimately leads a person in a moral path, for good or ill, it requires schooling. Aristotle explains in the *Nicomachean Ethics* that, to become virtuous, it is necessary 'to enjoy and be pained by the things we should' (1104b). In other words, the development of moral virtue entails the schooling of desire. Just as becoming a connoisseur of fine wines or acquiring a taste for culinary delicacies requires a gradual process of educating one's palate, becoming a virtuous person – a connoisseur of life – involves desiring what is truly worthwhile. And just as the university is the place where students are challenged to develop intellectual 'tastes' that are more mature, nuanced and refined, it should also be a place where students are prompted to refine and, if necessary, redirect their desires.

Before going any further, it would be helpful here to clarify the distinction between moral and intellectual virtue, as both need to be developed in tandem. Properly speaking, the moral virtues such as self-mastery, temperance and courage relate more specifically to the education of our desires, while the intellectual virtue of practical wisdom or prudence enables us to act in particular circumstances so as to attain the good that we desire. The moral and intellectual virtues are closely interrelated. Concerned with particulars of action, practical wisdom is absolutely necessary in order to determine how to act in specific circumstances, or in Aristotle's words, 'to know what is good for oneself' (1142a). Aristotle even goes so far as to say that 'without prudence virtues cannot exist', but that where there is prudence, 'all the others are present' (1144b). Prudence and ethical virtue are in fact inseparable, much like two sides of the same coin: 'a man cannot be good in the main sense without prudence, nor can he be prudent without ethical virtue' (1144a). A person lacking in prudence would be incapable of putting good desires into effect. Conversely, a person with unschooled or poorly schooled desires will not be prudent, even if he or she can recite Aristotle's *Nicomachean Ethics* by heart.

To help students become more virtuous, therefore, we need to do more than just offer courses that teach about moral theories. We need to find ways to refine students' desires, to prompt students to *want* to lead a virtuous life, a life that is directed towards a genuinely worthy purpose.

Some may object that, by the time students enter the university, their character is already basically formed, for good or for ill. And it is true that the habits developed in childhood and early adolescence have a huge impact on the development of character. If, as Aristotle says, the moral dispositions and habits developed 'from our early youth' make 'all the difference' in our ability to become virtuous adults, perhaps by the time students enter college it is too late to make a significant impact on their character (1103b25). Yet there are countless examples of individuals – Augustine in his *Confessions*, Sydney Carton in *Tale of Two Cities*, Raskolnikov in *Crime and Punishment* – who failed to develop good moral habits, but whose dramatic moral turnaround was brought about by pivotal life experiences, suffering, joys and relationships with others.[4]

Further, an improved scientific understanding of human development indicates that college may in fact be the perfect time to teach students about virtue. In his article on moral education at the university level, Professor Brian Jorgenson of Boston University cites studies demonstrating that a second state of brain development occurs in the late teens and early twenties, during which the frontal lobes and

---

4. I explore these factors that bring about morally pivotal points in the lives of fictional protagonists in my book, *Teaching Character Education Through Literature: Awakening the Moral Imagination* (RoutledgeFalmer 2004).

subcortical areas of the brain mature. These areas are associated, respectively, with abstract thought and with memory, attention and emotional control. University students are, therefore, at a particularly impressionable stage in their lives. At the same time, the nature of the college experience – a rite of passage in which most students leave home for the first time and are free to either accept or reject the values of their families – makes it a morally pivotal stage in most students' lives. A university can aspire to provide the rich array of questions, challenges and experiences that will prompt young adults to develop those habits of mind and character that will enable them to desire and pursue worthy goals.

In many ways, Plato's allegory of the cave vividly illustrates both the difficulty and the importance of character education for university students. In his revision of G. M. A. Grube's translation of the *Republic*, C. D. C. Reeve (1992) introduces the allegory by explaining, 'Socrates makes it clear that the aim of education is to turn the soul around by changing its desires' (p. 186). Desires change, we learn, in response to a change or refinement in one's goals or aspirations. These aspirations are akin to the Greek notion of *telos*, an ultimate end, or moral vision that lends coherence to one's desires and commitments. A *telos* embraces an intended conception of happiness; it is that overarching 'worthy purpose' of which Helen Keller speaks. The cave is essentially an allegory about the soul's being awakened to, seeing, and then moving towards a refined *telos* based no longer on deceptive shadows, but on truth. It is a story of liberation. The university years undoubtedly constitute a time in which young adults are forming, changing or refining their aspirations. The question that Plato's cave analogy presents is whether these students will embrace a *telos* that is really worthwhile, or whether their aspirations will remain limited by a superficial vision of reality.

The image that Socrates offers is of imprisoned persons deep within a cave, forced to face a wall upon which shadows cast from objects passing in front of a fire behind them serve as the only reality they know. To see the actual 'artifacts' being carried by unknown passersby and projected by the firelight onto the wall, they need to be freed from their chains and turn to face the light of the fire. To see further, to understand who these passersby are, where they come from, and what they carry, they must venture towards the light of the sun and begin an arduous ascent from the cave to the unfamiliar world outside. Because their eyes are not accustomed to the light, each turn and movement towards the sun evinces pain. Moreover, the steep climb demands rigorous effort. It is more comfortable to turn away from the light of the fire, to avoid the rigours of the ascent, and the blinding light of the sun, and to stay immersed in the darkness of the cave facing the familiar shadows on the wall. Yet to avoid the ascent and remain content with images is to deny reality, to live complacently in ignorance of the truth.

In the prisoners captivated by the perhaps alluring but deceptive shadows on the wall, I believe that we find a metaphorical representation of many college students. In his article 'Organization Kid', Brooks (2001) describes today's college students, especially those at elite universities, as unique precisely because of their *lack* of rebellion against the prevailing societal standards. During a visit to Princeton, Brooks spoke with Fred Hargadon, the Dean of Admissions, about the character of Princeton's students. Brooks found that Hargadon, 'like almost all of the other older people I talked to, is a little disquieted by the achievement ethos and the calm acceptance of established order that prevails among elite students today'. Having grown up in an era of prosperity, these students do not want to challenge this 'meritocratic system', in which one's worth is determined by one's resume, GPA and professional achievement. Instead, they work industriously to continue building their resumes and preparing themselves to make steady progress towards professional success. For these students, explains Brooks, education is not about seeking the truth or exploring new ways of thinking about life, but is rather one more step on the ladder towards success.

While Brooks does not condemn this attitude completely, he believes that it has a 'dark side' because it stifles intellectual creativity and deep reflection on any one subject. Students know that in this meritocratic system 'they are rewarded for mastering the method of being a good student, not for their passion for the content of any particular area of learning. They are rewarded for their ability to mindlessly defer to their professor's wishes, and never strike out on their own or follow a contradictory path' (Brooks, 2002). As he travelled to different universities and spoke with students, Brooks met 'students who felt compelled to do summer internships at investment banks and consulting groups because the system subtly encourages that kind of ascent-oriented summer job,…students who had a secret passion for philosophy, but who majored in economics under the mistaken impression that economics represents a higher step up the meritocratic ladder'. Overall, Brooks observes that the students he met 'had never really thought about how they wanted to spend their lives. They had never really used their imagination to create an ideal future.' In her article, 'Rekindling meaning in undergraduate education', Susan Ambrey cites Ellen Condliffe Lagemann, Dean of the Harvard Graduate School of Education, who believes that higher education 'has become more focused on technical and professional education than it was in the 1970s'. Lagemann laments that 'we are graduating students who are either narrowly focused on "vocational preparation" or who have attended "seemingly directionless programs of liberal study"'.[5] The problem, argues Brooks (2002), is that 'this vast meritocratic system has a huge hole at the end of it'. In other words, it lacks a genuine *telos*, the worthy purpose that is crucial for genuine happiness.

Much like the prisoner's in Plato's cave, students like those Brooks described need to be challenged to reflect more deeply on reality – to seek the ultimate truths of which the shadows on the wall are but a reflection or distortion. Education as conceived by Plato is precisely the 'journey' that 'awaken[s] the best part of the soul [reason] and lead[s] it upward to the study of the best things among the things that are' (*Republic* VII, 532b5). It is about the soul's movement from the visible realm – what one can physically see and know immediately (the shadows) – to the intelligible realm – what one can understand – to wisdom itself. This turning of the soul and movement towards the intelligible takes a determined effort, a desire to see and know what is really fundamental – not simply what strikes a superficial observer.

In exploring the schooling of desire, we are, in Plato's words, 'investigating something of supreme importance, namely the good and bad life' (*Republic* IX, 578c). Throughout his dialogues, Plato suggests that the soul is fundamentally erotic and propelled naturally

---

5. Ambrey is quoting from: Lagemann, E. C. (Spring 2003). The challenge of liberal education: Past, present, and future. *Liberal Education*, 89, 2, 6–13.

by desire or guided with assistance from a teacher. Education in its broadest sense helps us to rise above our present circumstances. The schooling of desire, then, presupposes the soul's motion – progress towards a superior point of view (a refined *telos*) and way of being.

How is this progress, this clarity of vision or understanding achieved? How can a professor prompt or awaken his or her students' desire to achieve this vision? In other words, how can professors help students to develop both intellectual and moral virtue?

Socrates or Protagoras? the professor as moral educator

Let's look to Plato again as he shows us Socrates engaged in the kind of teaching that refines his student's vision and desire. In the *Protagoras*, Socrates points to the primacy of education in our lives; it penetrates the very core of our being, our soul. He advises Hippocrates, therefore, to 'consider carefully' and make an informed judgement before entrusting his soul to the renowned sophist, Protagoras. Socrates makes the following exhortation to his young interlocutor, Hippocrates:

> Do you see what kind of danger you are about to put your soul in? If you had to entrust your body to risk it becoming healthy or ill, you would consider carefully whether you should entrust it or not. . . . But when it comes to something you value more than your body, namely, your soul, and when everything concerning whether you do well or ill in your life depends on whether it becomes worthy or worthless, I don't see you getting together with your father or brother or a single one of your friends to consider whether or not to entrust your soul to this newly arrived stranger. (313abc)

Submitting oneself to any education without an understanding of the *telos* of that education – where it will lead a person and how it will improve one's soul – Socrates suggests, is not only irresponsible, but also potentially deleterious to one's psychic health.

It is desire that incites the young Hippocrates to pound on Socrates' door, awaken him before dawn, and enlist his support as an intercessor before the renowned sophist, Protagoras. Hippocrates is desirous on many levels – he is enslaved by his appetites, but he also clearly desires wisdom – both the wisdom of Socrates to whom he appeals for help most immediately and the wisdom of Protagoras whose fame precedes him. He tells Socrates that Protagoras has a 'monopoly on wisdom' and that he is willing to 'bankrupt' himself and his friends in order to gain some of Protagoras' wisdom and fame (310e). Through his dialogue with Socrates, Hippocrates' desires undergo a particular schooling; his vision is refined. How does dialogue evoke a salutary change in his desires? How does Socrates challenge him to examine the worthiness of his aspirations?

In the context of a trusting relationship and a simple conversation, Socrates urges Hippocrates to be reflective, to seek advice from family and friends, to pursue what is good for his soul. Thus, Plato shows us that discernment of what is good requires intersubjectivity – the engagement of two souls in dialogue, one leading the other with questions. The questions themselves emerge from the ordinary, immediate and particular circumstances and claims of the interlocutor. They are not unwarranted or contrived to trip up the individual being questioned. Rather, they relate to practical concerns and gently lead the soul up the inclined plane to reflective engagement. Dialectic helps the interlocutor identify and reconcile conflicting claims and desires within his soul.

Thus the conversation between Socrates and Hippocrates illustrates the schooling of desire. The process of subjecting one's claims to investigation involves not simply a concern for truth but a concern for the individual soul – in this case Hippocrates – who has (consciously or unconsciously) chosen to place himself in Socrates' care. In the *Protagoras* Socrates does not ride roughshod over souls; instead he illustrates that Socratic education is 'person-centred'; Socrates attends to Hippocrates' soul.[6] Their exchange is familiar and even playful. Socrates recognizes Hippocrates' spiritedness and wants to learn what he is 'made of' (311b). Socrates knows he has to calm Hippocrates' blind enthusiasm, so he continues the conversation while strolling around the courtyard. He slows Hippocrates down

---

6. Socrates as a teacher, Teloh (1986) contends (1) 'looks at the nature of his subject, (2) observes how it can be made excellent, (3) looks for the means to engender its improvement' (14).

just long enough for him to reflect on his ambitions before rushing off to see Protagoras.

Socrates begins his work with Hippocrates by questioning his desire to study with Protagoras: 'But what is he, and what do you expect to become?' He walks Hippocrates through a series of analogies to help him articulate the determinate good he hopes to acquire from Protagoras. Socrates wants to help Hippocrates to develop understanding, to give an intelligent account of his ambition.

When Socrates finally presses Hippocrates on what he 'expects to become by going to Protagoras', he blushes at admitting 'a sophist' (312a). The daylight which dramatically 'show[s] him up' marks the beginning of Hippocrates' ascent to self-knowledge. He realizes that his goal is not as admirable as he had thought. Hippocrates is ashamed of his aspiration to become a sophist like Protagoras. Shame, the Greeks contend, is sometimes an important condition for learning and moral growth.[7] In the context of this dialogue, it incites the schooling of desire in Hippocrates. Socrates helps Hippocrates to consider what it is, in fact, that he is seeking from an education under Protagoras. Thus, Hippocrates grows in understanding and his capacity to see. As Losin (1996) points out, 'Genuine understanding is articulate or at any rate articulable: Plato is unwilling to credit anyone with understanding who cannot give or defend an account of that which he claims to understand' (p. 59). Hippocrates comes to realize that he is unable to defend his claim that he will gain wisdom by studying under Protagoras. He becomes aware of his own ignorance, that he does not know why he is willing to surrender his soul to Protagoras. Thus, Socrates incites Hippocrates' desire to know the true end of his quest for wisdom. Through dialectical inquiry, Socrates effectively redirects Hippocrates' desire from a blind desire to acquire Protagoras' fame to a refined desire to discern the wisdom that truly nourishes the soul (313d). Socrates has invited Hippocrates to consider the merit of his desires.

Hippocrates' untutored desires at the opening of the dialogue amount to personal enslavement blinding him from a vision beyond the transitory particulars of a materially successful life. Plato shows

---

7. In his Nicomachean Ethics, Aristotle categorized shame as the quasi-virtue of the learner (IV. 9, 1128b12 and also X. 9).

us that the dialectical path is educatively salutary: it schools desire by elevating and pointing it towards its proper *telos*.[8] Simply put, dialectic prompts the soul to attend to what is most worthwhile. Authentic moral education – the schooling of vision and desire – demands a courageous pursuit of the highest ideal and, ultimately, satisfies the soul.[9]

Too many of our students are like Hippocrates, except that they want to be doctors, teachers, scientists, MBAs or CEOs rather than sophists, and they have no idea why, or their reasons are superficial. The fast track to success and self-realization prevalent in our culture can deceive students as well as professionals into believing that as soon as they earn a degree they will be happy. They will have their ticket to personal success. Their eager pursuit of success is instigated by a culture of test prep, college application consultants, and an emphasis on resume-building that begins as early as elementary school. They have been brought up in, and are uncritical of, this meritocratic, achievement-driven system that Brooks describes in his articles.

Genuine happiness, however, depends less on our academic success, money and circumstances than it does on our virtue, our disposition to see well and choose wisely in all spheres of life. When we recognize what is worthwhile, we can choose to commit ourselves to a 'worthy purpose'. Viktor Frankl's insights are square with those of Helen Keller and Plato. Happiness, Frankl argues, is not something we find by pursuing it; rather it is something that 'ensues' from the pursuit of a worthy goal outside of ourselves. What we really need, he explains, is not happiness in the abstract but rather a 'reason to be happy'. Hippocrates blindly pursued the fame and fortune he believed he would enjoy if he followed Protagoras. With the refined vision evoked by his conversations with Socrates, he is more capable of choosing the pursuit of true wisdom over the pursuit of fame.

What is the average university student's understanding of happiness? It can amount to getting good grades, staying out of trouble,

---

8. '[W]hen the eye of the soul is really buried in a sort of barbaric bog, dialectic gently pulls it out and leads it upwards' (Republic VII, 533b; d).
9. Diotima speaks of this pursuit in the Symposium:
Look ... at how human beings seek honor. You'd be amazed at their irrationality ... wanting to become famous and 'to lay their glory forever.' ... I believe that anyone will do anything for the sake of immortal virtue and the glorious fame that fallows; and better the people the more they will do because they are in love with immortality (208 DE).

enjoying oneself, experiencing high adventure, taking risks, learning as much as possible, making friends, satisfying whims, leading a fully flourishing life or some combination of all of these. Virtue is needed, however, to help students adjudicate among competing claims about what will make them happy, that is, to help them discover what is really desirable.

It is unfair to stereotype or categorize students, but perhaps there are two extremes that serve to illustrate the spectrum of desires students bring with them to their college or university. Some come without any clear goals or sense of direction, let alone a vision for their lives as a whole. These hope to discover something worth investing themselves in during their college years. The other extreme arrives at the university with a predetermined career path, including a plan for graduate study or professional training and a fervent desire to reach that goal. We have met the student who is enamoured of free floating – exploring different fields and unwilling to commit by the end of sophomore year. We are also familiar with the driven pre-med or early childhood education major who cannot be persuaded to experiment with a course that might take her 'off track'.

While the vast majority of students we meet fall somewhere in the middle, it is also true that many undergraduate students do not see how their goals or developing goals fit into a larger scheme or vision of their lives as a whole. In short, college students tend to have unfocused goals or technical career goals, but rarely a vision for their lives as a whole. A greater vision is essential, however, if they are to endure the stresses of college life, and manage leisure, to withstand the allures of an entertainment-rich, media-saturated and consumer-driven society. University students need to learn to navigate their freedom well, and university professors can help them do that.

Yet when students enter the doors of our universities or classrooms, whom do they encounter: Protagoras or Socrates? As compared with the universities of the early 1900s, universities today tend to resemble in many ways the education offered by Protagoras much more than that offered by Socrates. To take Princeton as one example, Brooks observes in 'Organization Kid' that the members of the old elite 'were relatively unconcerned with academic achievement but went to enormous lengths to instill character. We, on the other hand, place enormous emphasis on achievement but are tongue-tied and hesitant when it comes to what makes for a virtuous life.' Ambrey (2004), Vice Provost for Undergraduate Education at Oakland University, similarly notes that attempts to engage in character education at the university frequently meet strong resistance from the faculty, springing from a mistaken understanding of Enlightenment ideals. As Princeton Professor Jeffrey Herbst commented, 'We've taken the decision that these are adults and this is not our job. There's a pretty self-conscious attempt not to instill character' (Brooks, 2001).

Compare Awbrey and Herbst's observations to this excerpt from John Hibben's address to Princeton's graduating students in 1913:

> You, enlightened, self-sufficient, self-governed, endowed with gifts above your fellows, the world expects you to produce as well as to consume, to add to and not to subtract from its store of good, to build up and not tear down, to ennoble and not degrade. It commands you to take your place and to fight your fight in the name of honor and of chivalry, against the powers of organized evil and of commercialized vice, against the poverty, disease, and death which follow fast in the wake of sin and ignorance, against all the innumerable forces which are working to destroy the image of God in man, and unleash the passions of the beast. There comes to you from many quarters, from many voices, the call of your kind. It is the human cry of spirits in bondage, of souls in despair, of lives debased and doomed. It is the call of man to his brother . . . such is your vocation; follow the voice that calls you in the name of God and of man. The time is short, the opportunity is great; therefore, crowd the hours with the best that is in you.
>
> (Brooks, 2001)

Of course, in an age of pluralism and diversity, it may be unrealistic – perhaps even undesirable – for most universities to teach virtue in such an explicit way. Yet it is also impossible to remain entirely neutral on the question of character. By showing no real concern for students' character – and emphasizing perfect test scores, high GPAs and crammed resumes instead – universities send an implicit message that achievement is more important than virtue.

It is also interesting to note, in stark contrast to the universities of a century ago, the absence of attempts to instill a sense of social obligation among students, and the relative apathy among students with regard to civic and political life. There are, naturally, always exceptions, and I do not mean to generalize that the vast majority of university students are politically apathetic. The observations below are more descriptive than prescriptive in nature. In my own students, I have seen a growing spirit of altruism over the last several years, an eagerness to participate in service programmes at home or abroad, to assist in relief efforts, build homes, volunteer in shelters. Altruism aside, political and civic activism does seem to have waned, but I cannot draw firm conclusions based on limited data. It does seem that there has been a shift from the time when the best and brightest students aspired to achieve prominent positions in politics to today's elite who aspire to become CEOs or corporate consultants. Former Harvard President Bok (2004) is troubled by the decline in civic responsibility among university students:

> We know from annual surveys that college freshman have less interest in politics now than they have had at any time since those surveys began in the mid-60's. It's an interesting fact that high school dropouts of my generation, those over 65 years of age, vote much more than college graduates today under 30. The biggest decline in political participation during the last 20 years has been among college graduates.

While universities even up until more recent times had been hotbeds for political movements, with dining halls full of passionate conversation about controversial social and political issues, today 'students have no time to read newspapers, follow national politics, or get involved in crusades'. As one student journalist explained to Brooks (2001), '"People are too busy to get involved in larger issues. When I think of all that I have to keep up with, I'm relieved there are no bigger compelling causes…"'.

While it may make for quieter campuses and fewer disciplinary problems, this relative political apathy among students is disconcerting when considering the health of the country as a whole. It seems that this apathy finds its roots not only in the materialistic achievement ethos of today's consumer culture but also in the relativistic approach towards ethics that reigns supreme in contemporary universities. When students are told not only by the media but also by their professors that morality is a matter of sentiment, that two contradictory positions on an issue can be equally valid, that tolerance is more important than truth, and that political correctness must be upheld at all costs – when they are told, in other words, that they should not try to see beyond the shadows on the wall of the cave because it could seem intolerant, or because in fact there is no truth to find – it is no wonder that they no longer consider any cause compelling enough to warrant their devotion. Aristotle argues in Book One of *The Politics* that the ability to deliberate rationally about the nature of justice and its requirements in one's own society is essential not only for the health of the polis but also for the flourishing of each citizen. Universities have a key role to play in forming students who have a sense of civic responsibility, and who are capable of rational deliberation about ethical issues.

However, while this chapter deals with the importance of the aspirations of a university and a university education to instil character in students, the focus here is more how individual professors can and ought to develop the vision, critical judgement and good dispositions that will enable them to flourish as human beings and to make a positive contribution to society.

Faculty advisors have an obvious responsibility to help students make wise academic choices. For example, they may help an undecided student arrive at a particular academic major, or at least reduce the number of options. But for those students whom we are not advising or who are not majoring in the classes we teach, what compelling reasons do we give them (or illustrate for them by way of example, dialogue and learning experiences) for why our subject is meaningful, a rich complement to their life? How do we help them to see how this particular course or major subject fits into a good life? What can we do to help all of our students – majors and non-majors, focused and unfocused, and the myriad in between – see more clearly? How can we help our students, as Socrates helped Hippocrates, to begin to think about who they want to be and not just what they want to do?

Students can choose among a number of honourable paths. But dishonourable and utilitarian options also present themselves to them in many attractive incarnations. Choices based on utility are not bad in themselves but they do not necessarily invite students to stretch intellectually or personally. Socrates could have let Hippocrates simply follow Protagoras and pursue his desire for public fame. Students who are more interested in knowing what is going to be in an exam and the minimum requirements for the course are perhaps thinking more about what they have to do and less about who they want to become. We may find ourselves frustrated and impatient with students who insist on knowing the 'bottom line'. I am always a little taken aback when a student candidly interjects, 'Well, I'm trying to figure out what *you* want', in the middle of our discussing a paper.

There are many incarnations of Protagoras today, visions of happiness and success for which young people are willing to bankrupt themselves and passionately pursue. PBS Frontline aired a powerful programme, 'The Merchants of Cool', pointing out the forces driving the media's unrelenting marketing campaign targeted at teenagers. The online teacher's guide accompanying the programme invites us to question these 'creators and sellers of popular culture', by asking, '[A]re they simply reflecting teen desires or have they begun to manufacture those desires in a bid to secure this lucrative market?' (Rogow, 2001: 2). When we invite students to examine the content and worthiness of their desires, we help them to exercise intelligent choice in all spheres of life.

When we cut the deal, when we settle for their interest in the bottom line; when we don't challenge our students to assess the worthiness of their purposes and goals; when we give in, we allow our students to actively pursue misguided ideals. We give in when we neglect to challenge the limited vision of the student who is apparently on track to a respectable job but who has not thought about what it takes to be on track to happiness.

As professors what provisions do we make in our classrooms (lecture, section, labs and assignments) to slow our students down, to prompt thoughtful consideration? Socrates calmed the anxious Hippocrates and challenged him to give an account of his goals and desires. Socrates engages Hippocrates in a dialogue that provoked self-examination and a reevaluation of the goal on which he had set his heart. How often do we invite students to reflect on what they expect to get from their university education as a whole? How do we challenge them to look beyond the degree or the string of adventures they have had with roommates and friends? Do we invite them to consider how the course we teach and the papers and projects we assign contribute to their education as persons? We can teach virtue and increase students' chances for discovering a 'reason to be happy', as Frankl put it, to the extent that we help them subject their choices and aspirations (as well as those of others – fictional or real individuals whom we study) to rigorous reflection and thoughtful examination.

To take education in virtue seriously at the university, we also need to strive to live our own lives virtuously, to subject our own desires to investigation. In 'Socrates, Virtue and the Modern Professor', L. J. Samons II argues that a professor's ability to teach virtue rests largely on a professor's *being* virtuous. Samons cites Socrates as someone who was able to have such a profound effect on the lives of his students primarily because of his own example: 'to the extent that Socrates was able to *teach virtue* to and inspire his followers, he succeeded as much through the example of his life as through his views about piety or his theory of eternal Forms'. We run the risk as professors who are evaluated by (sometimes ruthless) students semester after semester of becoming more like Protagoras than like Socrates. We too can try to win students' attention by impressing them with our rhetorical skill and reputation. Dialogue and enquiry are crucial to the cultivation of virtue; posturing and politicking are not.

Just as our students' choices disclose their motivations and priorities for learning, our choices disclose our purpose and priorities in teaching. Are we really concerned about the well-being of our students, or do we think of teaching responsibilities as a burden that hampers our 'real' work of research and writing, and try to spend as little time as possible dealing with students? This may be especially difficult when we are under the real or apparent pressure to write and publish books and articles. And while research and writing are an essential part of our work – and also offer new insights for teaching – a balance needs to be achieved. Students can tell when professors care about their teaching and when they don't, and they are usually eager to interact with professors who take a personal interest in them as students. Maintaining a positive attitude towards teaching – seeing it as a scholarly and interpersonal pursuit with our students – and encouraging students to continue our conversation with them outside of formal class times are essential if we want to be able to foster the level of intellectual exchange with our students that Socrates had with Hippocrates.

When we challenge our students to penetrate the surface of things, to experience awe before the solar system or to revel in the wit and wisdom of Jane Austen; when the themes, principles and practical insights we disclose through our teaching prompt them to examine what they understand, what they believe and who they are, then we are pointing them in the right direction and helping to school their desires. As professors we must keep our sights high, staying focused not merely on our students' performance but also on the kinds of persons they are becoming. If we do, we will not only be helping our students to direct their lives towards a worthy purpose but also helping ourselves to do the same.[10]

---

10. I am grateful to Dr Moira Walsh for her instructive criticisms and response to an earlier version of this chapter and to Melissa Moschella for her research assistance.

Chapter 8

The character of higher education

Dennis Hayes

Every generation has its educational crisis. In seeking to determine what is considered worthwhile to transmit to the next generation, different educational values come into conflict. The fundamental opposition of values was put bluntly, but accurately, by John Anderson, who described education as a battlefield between *liberals*, who see any member of a new generation as 'the heir of all the ages', and *philistines* who merely see such individuals as 'job-fodder' (Anderson, 1980: 156). This opposition is familiar and for over two thousand years it has been the cause of anxiety and crisis for parents, teachers, politicians, philosophers and others concerned about future generations. In Aristotle's *The Politics*, for example, there is a description of anxiety and crisis that mirrors this concern in our contemporary writings on education, which are evident throughout the chapters in this book:

> in modern times there are opposing views about the tasks to be set, for there are no generally accepted assumptions about what the young should learn, either for virtue or for the best life; nor yet is it clear whether their education ought to be conducted with more concern for the intellect than for the character of the soul. The problem has been complicated by the education we see actually given; and it is by no means certain whether training should be directed at things useful in life, or at those conducive to virtue or at exceptional accomplishments. (All these answers have been

judged correct by somebody.) And there is no agreement as to what in fact
does tend towards virtue, so naturally they differ about the training for it.
(Aristotle, 1992, VIII ii 1337 a33: 453–454)

Nothing is new, then. Or is there something different about the early
twenty-first century crisis of education? James Arthur in his discussion
of 'character education' in schools hints at the difference by referring
to what he calls the 'litany of alarm' (2003: 3–5) about contemporary
youth. This litany focuses on the socially dysfunctional nature of this
new generation, which is said to result from a lack of social skills and
self-esteem. Hence the need for 'character education'. However, his
counter to scare stories about the depravity of youth is to indicate
that there *is* indeed nothing new, and he cites a savage murder of
a 72-year-old women by a 16-year-old in 1954, over the possible
discovery of a forged Scouting certificate, to make his point. Arthur
considers that the most valuable function of the litany is to help us
'fix our attention on how to effectively address the social and moral
problems of individuals and society' (2003: 5). Yet, out of the varied
accounts of responses he discusses, there is no solution to this contemporary malaise, merely an emphasis on the need for character
education, about the nature of which there is no consensus and much
confusion. We seem to really be at a social impasse that is something
other than the universal and timeless anxiety about what to transmit
to future generations.

One thing that indicates the profound nature of this social impasse
is that the responsibility for 'character education' has been relocated
from the home and church – we might like to add the workplace and
labour organization – to the school (Arthur, 2003: 147). This relocation
is not an insignificant change. It is one of the most important indicators
of societal failure. Perhaps an indicator of the significance of this relocation can be gleaned from Gerald Grace's reminder that historically
character education was associated with the religious and moral
indoctrination and 'schooling' for the purposes of upholding the British
class system (Grace, 2003: x). How is it that a bad thing has now
become represented as a good thing?

The litany of alarm about 'values' is part of a litany of loss that
is conscious of something missing but that has nothing to replace
what is lost. It is not just a matter of emphasis to note that the wider

community no longer ensures the transmission of values to the future generations and that this task is now to be undertaken by educational institutions, whether they are schools, colleges or universities. It is an indication of a fundamental and unique historical disjuncture in which socialization is becoming the prime function of educational institutions. The relocation of socialization to institutions reflects the crisis of moral authority in society. A formal intervention by a state institution is now necessary to replace the informal networks and relationships that taught values and trust between people. It may seem merely uncontentious to emphasize 'values' in educational institutions, but in the context of the lack of moral authority, the consequence is profound. Socialization is being substituted for education.

The influence of crude sociology on our thinking is such that it might seem that educational institutions, particularly schools, were always key players in the process of socialization. What this banal observation ignores is the significance of the shift. Even not so long ago as 1954, their prime function was education, and socialization was just something they did, largely for the reasons mentioned by Grace, and the best and less docile pupils resisted and despised this part of their 'schooling'. What we are seeing is a reversal of the traditional situation. At school and college, pupils and students increasingly get socialization first, and whatever education they receive is peripheral, almost an accidental add-on to their social training.

This situation might be welcomed by religious and moral conservatives, often in alliance with 'radical' or progressive educationalists, as a chance to promote particular values or sets of values, but it is a fragile and self-defeating reversal. It is not a social advance but an artificial attempt to replace what has been lost in wider society. Artificiality, disguised as innovation, is a defining feature of what are sometimes called 'third-way' policies and practices. 'Character education' is a good example of a third-way initiative. Like all others, it is doomed to failure because all attempts to impose sets of values on young people will be fragile outside of what is often a 'consensus' but actually means a web of meaning in which these values make sense. What we face is not the traditional conflict about which values to transmit but a situation that is characterized by the absence of values. 'Character', as Richard Sennett reminds us, is rooted in knowledge, values and practices that develop over time, whether at work, in the community or at school (Sennett, 1998). Once these knowledge, values and practices have gone or been destroyed, politicians cannot simply plan to reactivate or replace them. If social practices and communities disintegrate, they cannot be regenerated, as a disused parking lot can be, by outside intervention. New communities and values have to develop spontaneously over time. But politicians and moralists show a deep distrust for ordinary people and would rather intervene. Once this was because they felt they knew better than others, whereas today it is simply because they have the power to intervene. Education is now the last societal institution where there can be a direct relationship between government and people. Hence the slogan 'education, education, education', which does not express a renewed interest in education but merely articulates the political bankruptcy of our time. One result of these 'third way' interventions is that educationalists find themselves on the central political stage and it is flattering. They are easily engaged in political projects such as 'education for citizenship' or, indeed, 'character education'. We can add many other 'subjects' such as 'environmental' education to the list. Educationalists may feel their hour has come and, mostly, they offer their unqualified support to these initiatives. The irony is that the more the state intervenes to impose 'character education', the very process of imposition undermines its objectives.

The value vacuum

The renewed emphasis on 'values' is the most confusing and most philosophical of recent political interventions that is, for the moment, taking the form of an interest in 'character education'. The discussions are often very abstract, something that does not reflect a renewed period of influence for philosophers of education but a fairly obvious retreat from an emphasis on content to an emphasis on form. The form of the traditional discussion about what to transmit to future generations is now empty of any content. There is no longer any real debate about opposing values, merely a vacuum. 'Values' are emphasized in a quite formal way that has ridiculous consequences. We have a situation in which all that happens is that there is an arbitrary reassertion of traditional values, or 'multicultural' values, or both at the same time! The confused and confusing litany of alarm is in reality an expression of political and social unease and distrust at the highest levels. To this extent Arthur is right; the 'youth' are probably as well behaved as ever they were. What is different is that those who control our lives have no clear values to offer. Almost any values will do.

Contemporary writers on 'character education' do not assert an agreed set of values as there is no consensus on what these should be. The question is not 'can virtues be taught?' but 'are there any virtues we still believe in that we can teach?' The overall climate is one of uncertainty. The only thing that is certain is that the one value that will not be emphasized is the pursuit of knowledge. Even Arthur, in concluding his thorough survey of character education, rejects current educational eclecticism, therapeutic education *and* the Socratic belief that Knowledge is Virtue (2003: 146). This latter rejection seems self-defeating even for his own project of moving young people away from self-interest to a concern for others. If this is to be no more than another fragile belief in the possibility of inculcating social altruism in the young, it must be grounded in the prioritizing of knowledge over other values. Knowledge may not be virtue but it certainly is *a* virtue. It is the pursuit and acquisition of knowledge that holds out the only possibility of transcending self-absorption.

This is the crucial issue in discussions of values and 'character education'. If the pursuit of knowledge is becoming universally side-lined in favour of other values this is tantamount to a rejection of the modern educational project that, in schools and, most importantly, in the university, has existed for the last 150 years, if not since the Enlightenment.

In discussing 'character education' in relation to the university, the modern, not the traditional, response is that it has no role whatsoever. The modern understanding of higher education is essentially that of Newman's *The Idea of a University* (1852). It is a place of 'teaching universal knowledge' and this implies that its object is 'intellectual, not moral' (Newman, 1852/1996: 3). We can disagree with Newman as to whether the university should be restricted to the diffusion and extension rather than the advancement of knowledge but this is not relevant here. Newman articulates the progressive and modern view of university in the same way as Arnold articulated a progressive and modern view of education, or initiation into culture, as enabling new generations to learn '*the best that is known and thought in the world*' (1864/ 2002: 50). These are marvellous, concise expressions of what education is about, *teaching universal knowledge* and not in any way everyday or practical knowledge (skills) but *the best* that is known and thought in the world. When they are referred to today, which is hardly ever, they are not commonplace remarks, but reminders of what is under threat not merely from government intervention but from the uncertainty of academics and teachers about the value of knowledge.

The concern with education and ethics in higher education is not a positive development. In the contemporary context it undermines the ideal and the actuality of the university. The only virtue appropriate to the university is the pursuit of knowledge. Other virtues may be important but they have no place being promoted in the university. As we shall see, there are values other than the epistemological values that a commitment to truth implies, but these are not merely secondary but contingent values.

The contemporary crisis of education

Anderson saw the traditional or universal crisis of education as broadly concerned with the conflict between the pursuit of knowledge and training for a job. 'Character education', as we have been reminded, was traditionally conceived of as a training in docility and compliance. The form that the contemporary crisis of education takes is to represent all forms of social training as an educational project. 'Knowledge' drops out of the picture all together. The abandonment of knowledge as a virtue in an educational context mirrors a lack of political confidence. It is the pursuit of knowledge that drives society forwards. For the first time in modern history that belief is failing along with other beliefs.

The consequence of this failing belief is that society and individuals emphasize self-limitation over individual potential and achievement (Furedi, 2003: 21). This self-limitation may coexist with a psychological state of self-absorption or narcissism encouraged by anxious elites all too happy to explain away their anxiety and lack of values by blaming ordinary people and youth in particular. By downplaying knowledge we limit education and limit the possibility of self-development. 'Character education' initiatives and explorations take place in a situation where a diminished sense of self exists. It is a sociological platitude that we live in a more individualized and atomized society, but what is ignored is that contemporary invidualization bears no resemblance to the aggressive, rugged Reaganite or Thatcherite individualism that was seen as a threat to a social responsibility just two decades ago. The new 'individual' is a much more vulnerable subject seen and often willing to be seen as unable to cope and needing help. Even going to university, one of the safest places on earth, is now considered traumatic for even the most intelligent and affluent individuals (Furedi, 2003: 108). Never before did so many students come for interview with their parents and feel the need for induction courses and even support and counselling to cope with leaving home. As a result, a new sort of impoverished individual is being responded to and also formed by the university.

The existence of this new and diminished self, with its spontaneous concern with self-limitation, hints at something ethical, but there is nothing ethical or positive in it at all. The ethical hint is towards Aristotelian ethics. Reading the lists of values mentioned in the discussion of character education it is difficult not to repeat, once again, Russell's summative judgement on the *Ethics*:

> Those who neither fall below nor rise above the level of decent, well-behaved citizens will find in the *Ethics* a systematic account of the principles by which they hold that their conduct should be regulated. Those who demand anything more will be disappointed. The book appeals to the respectable middle-aged, and has been used by them, especially since the seventeenth century, to repress the ardours and enthusiasms of the young. But to a man with any depth of feeling it is likely to be repulsive.
> (Russell, 1940: 195)

We can add the adjective anxious to 'middle-aged' respectables described in this passage and it does, in part, explain the appeal of Aristotle's thinking to writers on ethics and character. First, because it is essentially individualistic, requiring that individuals embody virtues and secondly, because 'these virtues represent median points between extremes' (Macfarlane, 2004: 37). Putting this formal point aside, resurrecting the requirement to embody virtues in one's behaviour seems merely an academic version of the current popular obsession with personality in politics and life. This obsession requires people to be dull or they will be judged not on their politics or abilities, but on their personal behaviour, and there is certainly an uninspiring catalogue of virtues in the literature for them to model, including: honesty, temperance, courage, fairness, friendliness, honour, shame, truthfulness and charity.

The Aristotelian view, now developing into the theory or theories known as 'virtue ethics', can be put in a nutshell as the view that you cannot be a good lecturer or teacher without being a good person. This is a viewpoint associated in recent times with the philosopher David Carr among others, who argues that 'A key factor for virtue ethicists is the modelling of conduct through the example of others' (Carr and Steutel, 1999: 253). Virtue ethics emphasizes the intrinsic worth of virtues such as those listed above. A similar list is adopted for higher education teachers by Macfarlane in his book *Teaching with Integrity* that adopts a virtue ethics approach to close what he sees as an ethical 'lost dimension' to teaching in higher education. This is his list, with the area of activity to which they apply in brackets: respectfulness (teaching), sensitivity (tutoring), pride (preparation), courage (innovation), fairness (assessment), openness (evaluation), restraint (ideology) and collegiality (managing) (Macfarlane, 2004: 128–129). The first impression made by this list is that, if these are the values that Macfarlane researched and presented as potentially constitutive of the personal 'integrity' that teachers in higher education require, they are mostly borrowed from the language of counselling and therapy. In Aristotelian fashion they exclude the very extremes that might make for exciting and passionate teaching. Let's take two examples, one that is not obviously a 'therapeutic' label and one that is. 'Restraint' is said to be the mean in 'Ideology' between evasiveness and self-indulgence. But in the account given we are told that although it is difficult to separate our passion from our 'ideological and intellectual prejudices' – whatever these are, presumably they refer to lecturers with a theoretical base to their arguments – we most avoid the tendency to be domineering rather than empowering (2004: 140–142).

We shouldn't proselytize or indoctrinate by taking advantage of the unequal power relationship in the classroom. But this is to reduce the university lecture or seminar to 'circle time' in the primary class-room. What Macfarlane calls domineering or proselytizing could be seen as merely the strongest advocacy of the truth, and even then a 'domineering' lecturer might find his ideas more readily challenged than a 'restrained' lecturer. Isn't it familiar enough to lecturers already that all too often students consider any forceful argument as 'indoctrination' or an example of academics being 'domineering'. This facile egalitarianism that equates opinion with knowledge is not something that is to be encouraged. Nor can we simply add 'this is my view but there are others'. Why be restrained at all? Shouldn't we argue for what is true and ask or demand that students accept the truth or challenge it, if they can? We can also query the easy assertion about the need to be 'empowering' in the lecture theatre or seminar. Isn't this another way of presenting an agnosticism or lack of belief as a value and to incline lecturers towards a relativistic acceptance of student opinions? What should be required of students is some hard thinking as they follow the argument or demonstration, and some intelligent, critical questioning. This is application to the work required in becoming a true student, not subjugation, for there is no meaningful 'power relationship' here. What is required for real 'empowerment' is that students submit to serious learning and study to do away with the vice of their gnorance. Think of great teachers, like Wittgenstein, who domineered and demanded and mostly *won* absolute loyalty from his students. It is hard to see which of these or any other of the teaching virtues would apply to him. He was, however, the living embodiment of the epistemological value of 'going the bloody hard way'.

'Sensitivity', another of Macfarlane's medians, is clearly a therapeutic value; it embodies a requirement that we get to know our students and their personal needs and circumstances. It is a mean between 'indifference' and 'favouritism'. But why should we accept this as a value, we are interested only in the academic development of our students. Is not the academic virtue here closer to 'indifference', although we might call it professional detachment or disinterestedness? We are not interested in student personal problems whether they affect learning or not. It is not that there is an army of 'student support' workers in every university to support them that allows 'indifference' to be the key virtue here. Before 'Student Services' existed students kept their self-respect and if they had problems they kept them quiet and if they knew something they studied it privately. Why should tutors now think it a positive virtue to pry into students' private lives? On a personal side I remember the end of a philosophy course when a middle-aged professional student came and thanked me for the class. He told me that over the last eight months while he was attending the course his wife was dying of a painful illness. It was the experience of gaining distance from his personal problems that helped him survive. All our tutorials had been devoted to the discussion of ideas.

It is interesting that Macfarlane suggests that the need for this rather arbitrary catalogue of virtues is necessary because of government pressure to accept new sorts of student and to turn towards professional education. But Aristotelian median points identification of this sort is a game, a sophistry. Certain values are assumed and then presented as they had added value as median points. We simply don't have to play this game. We can defend values without reference to any mean. In reality, median values are a prescription for accommodating to the self-limiting an impoverished individual that we want to see when we look at our students. Whether they really are like this or capable of achieving their full potential will depend on rejecting this ethical approach and returning to a defence of the pursuit of knowledge.

Before leaving the respectable Aristotle and his followers, it is worth noting that this treatment of him is not entirely fair. In the *Ethics* he says that 'for a human being ... the life in accordance with intellect is best and pleasantest, since this, more than anything, constitutes humanity. So this life will also be the happiest' (X. 7, 1178a Aristotle, 2000: 196). This is an extreme viewpoint and one that we could well adopt as an antidote to the current emphasis on both emotional education and 'character education.'

As all education is becoming socialization it is unsurprising that rather than stand as the last bastion of the enlightenment values of reason, truth and progress, it is in the university that we find its most dangerous and influential critics. These critics are not the bureaucrats but the academics most concerned with studying and promoting higher education. They are mostly philosophers of higher education and those who induct new teachers into the profession. That these are the critics of the university ironically reveals the value of the 'ivory tower' as a place set aside from everyday concerns in order to reflect upon and attempt to understand the world.

But before considering the critics, and one critic in particular, we must deal with an objection by the defenders of the university that indicates the true character of higher education and its 'values'.

Newman's 'sophistry'

There are only a few unequivocal defences of the traditional liberal view of the university as the quintessential modern institution that embodies the enlightenment belief in the pursuit of knowledge. Two are Gordon Graham's *Universities: The Recovery of an Idea* and Duke Maskell and Ian Robinson's *The New Idea of a University*. Both are committed to a view of the university that is not only related to, or inspired by, Newman but made more consistent and relevant to the contemporary world of higher education. Graham argues that in the university socialization has no place and 'the commitment to truth over usefulness is paramount' (2002: 122). However, he does accept that universities have a socially useful role in 'maintaining and continuously revitalizing cultural inheritances' (2002: 123). This means continuing study of the disciplines and supplying critical minds. Graham, here and elsewhere, argues that academics have no role in 'character education' or any other aspect of socialization.

Maskell and Robinson accuse Newman of sophistry in relation to his defence of a liberal education as something opposed to education for the professions. In particular, they cite a passage in the second edition which they say contains Newman's 'fraudulent promise' that universities have made to students ever since that 'cultivating disinterest is the way to many self-interested ends, [and] that an education that treats knowledge as its own remuneration will be very remunerative' (2002: 31) . This is the offending passage:

> that philosophical or liberal education, as I have called it, which is the proper function of a University, if it refuses the foremost place to professional interests, does but postpone them to the formation of the citizen, and, while it subserves the larger interests of philanthropy, prepares also for the successful

prosecution of those merely personal objects, which at first sight it seems to disparage.

(Newman, 1852/1996, VII 6: 119)

Newman is answering the 'fallacy' in the argument of John Locke, who believed that only professional training is useful. Maskell and Robinson make the claim that he achieves this because he uses an unintentional piece of sophistry. He changes the meaning of terms such as 'mental culture' and 'culture of the mind' from one passage to another: 'He slides from "the mind itself... mental nature... character" to "intellect... facilities... exercises of the mind... intellectual powers"' and is not far away from what trainers today call 'personal transferable skills' (2002: 31–32). Indeed, any reader of Newman is struck by the boldness of his claims that a liberal education makes for easy entry into and consequent success in the professions. Without rejecting Maskell and Robinson's critique of what Newman wrote, there is something true in what he argues and we can re-state this without slipping into defending 'personal transferable skills' or setting the foundations for 'character education' in higher education.

As well as the cultural inheritance passed on through a study of the disciplines at university, that Graham mentions, it is undeniably the case that as that study has generalizable epistemological elements or 'values', that these might or might not carry over and facilitate professional careers or enhance personal life. We may even hope that they do. Take Graham's central example of a commitment to truth. We might expect that this could lead to a contempt for lies, an unshakeable belief in being honest and a willingness to put up a coherent, courageous and vigorous defence of what we hold to be true, whatever the personal consequences. These 'values' derive from epistemology and make no sense without reference to it. Consider, as a parallel example, what passes for 'research ethics'. They are for the most part entirely redundant. As David Bridges has pointed out:

> many of the virtues and principles which have been offered as conditions for successful enquiry themselves require epistemological reference. A notion like honesty can have little meaning without some reference to truth. The kind of scholarly qualities of care and thoroughness which are picked out in accounts of intellectual virtue are logically attached to notions

of, for example, the comprehensiveness of data, the seeking of possible
contradictory evidence, faithfulness between reported accounts and documentary and other sources – all of which are wrapped up with important
epistemological principles relating to what provides warrant for belief.

(Bridges, 2003: 6)

What is essential to note is that this carry over to professional life
of these epistemological 'values' is contingent. We might want to
celibate it but without claiming that it is part of the justification of
a liberal university education. We can keep the consequences of a
liberal education separate from the justification of a liberal education,
whether or not Newman kept them apart. The carry over to professional
life of secondary epistemological values is merely an example of
something that may happen as a result of a liberal education that may
be professionally helpful but may not be so. A commitment to honesty
in any profession can just as easily lead to professional failure, as the
sacking of 'whistle bowers' shows, as to success.

As the pursuit of knowledge is qualified or rejected as the goal in
the university these epistemological 'values' that relate to the essence
of higher education must be weakened. Universities and academics
that reject knowledge as their core value begin to take an active part
in producing self-limiting, ignorant and ineffectual students. Although
it does not seem like this because what is on offer – socialization
rather than education – is dressed up as an innovative response to
a changing world.

Higher education as socialization

There are several influential writers on higher education who promote
therapeutic approaches to higher education teaching (e.g. Cowan,
1998; Rowland, 2000). The influence of their work is growing and is
learning increasingly significant. But it remains attached to an approach
that is centred on and continues to value the disciplines. The damage
that this does is internal through influencing new academics to
see the value of therapy. Macfarlane's view is an example of a more
mainstream approach. He adopts a hybrid of the therapeutic approach
and an entirely pragmatic response to contemporary changes in the

university. It sounds good (Aristotelian) common sense. The dangers posed by these enemies within the university are masked because of their obvious ethical orientations.

However, although he is often self-consciously equivocal, it is in the work of Ronald Barnett that we get the clearest statement of the shift from education to socialization in higher education. He declares that 'Knowledge and control are not, thankfully, available. (That belief partly led to Auschwitz.) What is both necessary and possible – just – is an enlightened societal self-monitoring' (Barnett, 2000: 68). To facilitate this, the university must re-organize itself around the 'uncertainty principle'. This will transform it into an institution that '(i) contributes to our uncertainty in the world (through its research and consultancy); (ii) helps us monitor and evaluate that uncertainty (through its work as a centre of critique); and (iii) enables us to live with that uncertainty, through both the operational capacities and the existential capacities it promotes (in its pedagogical activities)' (Barnett, 2000: 69). This is a vision of the 'therapeutic university'. An institution that makes students feel safe and secure, and does not challenge them at all. But can it be taken seriously? The value of Barnett's work is not necessarily that it is true but that it captures in an extreme and rhetorical form the mood of the times. 'Enabling us to live with uncertainty' – the blurb on the book is to 'revel in our uncertainty' – is a vision of a therapeutic higher education suited to a new generation of students of the sort we described earlier as self-limiting and impoverished individuals.

The ethics of 'niceness'

It is hard to get passionate about challenging and changing students who have a self-limiting and impoverished sense of what they can achieve. They might benefit from some 'domineering' but we are fearful of doing so. There is a reason for this.

Allan Bloom famously characterized today's students as 'nice'. He said:

> Students these days are, in general, nice. I choose the word carefully. They are not particularly moral or noble. Such niceness is a facet of democratic

character when times are good. Neither war nor tyranny nor want has hardened them or made demands on them. The wounds and rivalries caused by class distinction have disappeared along with any strong sense of class.... Students are free of most constraints, and their families make sacrifices for them without asking for much in the way of obedience or respect. Religion and national origin have almost no noticeable effect on their social life or their career prospects. Although few really believe in 'the system,' they do not have any burning sentiment that injustice is being done to them.... Students these days are pleasant, friendly and, if not great-souled, at least not particularly mean-spirited. Their primary preoccupation is themselves, understood in the narrowest sense.

(Bloom, 1988: 82–83)

We can question the validity of almost any of Bloom's sociological claims, but the picture he paints is a fair one. It is a long way from the picture of disaffected and dysfunctional youth portrayed in the 'litany of alarm'. A decade and a half later, the generation of students he was talking about are today's new academics and the 'ethical' value of *niceness* has become ubiquitous throughout higher education. We are all expected to be nice to one another if nothing else.

In his latest book Barnett suggests that being nice to one another could be the basis for rebuilding the university: 'the smile in the corridor...is a statement in favour of the ideals of the university, in favour of tolerance, reasonableness, generosity and a will to go on. It is, in its own way, a rebuke to the ideologists who would wreck the university and condemn it to narrow, intolerant and fractional inter- ests. This is certainly not enough to rescue the university but it is, at least, a start' (Barnett, 2003: 180). Learning to smile at one another as a way of rescuing the university sounds like a harmless witticism with which to end a book, but it is a suggestion that could be interpreted as having dangerous therapeutic overtones. It is not the ideologists who are going to wreck the university but those who would ask us to be 'nice' and to respect one another.

'Nice' describes something or someone that is pleasant, but insipid. Those few lecturers who are uncompromising in the defence of their hard won ideas and who defend the pursuit of knowledge in their disciplines are likely to be looked upon as epistemological dinosaurs rather than nice people. As Evans has argued, unpleasant as the old (male) academics were, they shine above today's lecturers (Evans, 2004). For today's lecturers, like today's students, are 'nice'. They are too nice. They are too kind to challenge one another and to challenge their students and as a consequence students are not stretched. The result of all this is a diminished academic who is full of respect for others, particularly students or fellow 'learners', as they are now called, but who lacks intellectual self-respect. And lacking *intellectual self-respect* themselves, they have replaced *intellectual* respect for their students by simple *respect* for students as 'people'. Lecturers see students not as potential equals in the pursuit of knowledge but as simple equals. In this sense it is not just rhetoric, but an important truth, that students are now at the centre of the university. However, neither students nor educators benefit from this.

With the collapse of belief in the value of knowledge, today's lecturers will spontaneously, because they are nice, adopt a *therapeutic ethic*. Building up the self-esteem of students will seem more acceptable than the psychological or electric shock of the Socratic *elenchus* which was meant, by revealing contradictions, to put the student into the confusion and panic of the *aporia*. It was not intended to leave the student in a state of confusion and uncertainty, and therefore be a basis for the application of therapy to remove this stunned state. The intention was to enable the student to move further along the path from false belief to knowledge. Today, lecturers, the *elenchus*, would be in danger of getting formal complaints and law suits, never mind some very bad student evaluations. Even a milder form of student questioning, described by Ryan as 'education by interrogation', requires an apprenticeship relation of the knowledgeable and knowing tutor and the student that is hardly imaginable today (2001: 78–86). Lecturers who no longer search for truth can only explore, through a process of respectful and gentle questioning, the opinions and feelings of their students.

The therapeutic ethic and 'virtue ethics' in higher education achieve the same ends, an uninspiring and colourless 'ethic', more properly an etiquette, of 'niceness'. This is what the confused dialogue with Aristotle finally results in, and the result is damaging to the university. 'Character education' in higher education, if pursued, can only be more damaging. Any imposition of values other than knowledge must undermine the university.

In attacking the ethic of 'niceness', I am not suggesting that academics should be gratuitously rude to one another and to students, but that they must assert the authority that derives from their knowledge and expertise in their field, and this will mean being critical and uncompromising, particularly in defence of the pursuit of knowledge in the university.

The inversion of the transaction between generations

By being nice and accepting the authority, or rather authenticity, of the student experience, and the authority, or rather authenticity, of the variety of views or 'perspectives', lecturers have slowly and voluntarily given up their academic authority. And we can only say that this state of affairs is largely their fault and cannot be explained by the supposed intellectual triumph of post-modernism or relativism, or by political cynicism or market forces. These are post-hoc excuses and evasions.

It is worth recalling that Oakeshott called education, and we can say higher education *in particular*, a 'specific transaction ... between generations of human beings in which newcomers to the scene are initiated into the world they are to inhabit' (1972: 19). And he adds: 'To be initiated into this world is learning to become human; and to move within it freely is being human ...' (1972: 47). His conclusion is a damning critique of the educational philistines, that 'To be without this understanding is to be, not a human being, but a stranger to the human condition' (1972: 21).

To Oakeshott this transaction was about human understanding and not about socialization or social integration. When society ceases to be serious about this transaction, he argued that 'education becomes the engagement to teach nothing' (1972: 48). Education has become socialization and even in higher education there is an 'engagement to teach nothing'.

This is the tragedy that today's lecturers, as a result of their respect for the views of others, in particular of their students, and because of their ethic of *niceness*, have participated in the inversion of the transaction between generations. Students are now initiated into nothing. It is accepted that they already 'know' as much as, or, to put it better, can 'feel' as well as, any academic. The lecturer can only offer a different but equally valid set of feelings or 'perspectives'. Sadly, the consequences of the lack of academic authority are not purely academic.

What today's lecturers *fail* to transmit to today's students, those students, many of whom will be future teachers and lecturers, will be *unable* to transmit to future generations. For they will *know nothing* worthy of transmission.

Chapter 9

Developing citizenship through international exchanges

Ian Davies, Mark Evans, Peter Cunningham, Gunilla
Fredriksson, Graham Pike, Hanns-Fred Rathenow,
Alan Sears, Felicitas Tesch and Pam Whitty

Introduction

Citizenship can be considered and practised as people meet and
work together. Universities as sites of citizenship (Council of Europe,
2000a,b) are well placed not only to promote valuable work within
their immediate context but also to bring people together through the
process of international exchanges. This chapter discusses the issues
arising from work undertaken through a project that was developed
as a response to the increasing demand for effective citizenship
education in the interdependent and multicultural societies of Canada
and of the European Community. We worked mainly with trainee
teachers but also with 'leisure time workers' and other graduates
with specialisms in a variety of fields, attempting to expose them to
new cultural perspectives on education and citizenship. We wanted
to help all those who would become involved in our project to be
more competent and confident in their roles as national and global
citizens.

We undertook three interconnected activities:

1. organizing conferences in citizenship education in Europe and in Canada (year 1);
2. school-based involvement in a country other than their own (years 2 and 3) moving 75 student teachers and 8 members of staff;
3. a programme of activities designed to increase awareness of citizenship issues in a variety of settings (political, cultural and social) and to encourage the practice of education for citizenship in their future careers (years 2 and 3).

We argued in our proposal to the European Union and to the Canadian government that the experience of working in an unfamiliar cultural and educational setting would encourage participants' reflection on the nature of citizenship and that a diverse range of activities would provide ideas and strategies to help them promote citizenship in the future. We suggested that there would be benefits for non-mobile students who would discuss and otherwise work with the mobile group. We worked collaboratively on this project co-operating across four countries and our own higher education institutions, with the support of one associate institution on both sides of the Atlantic (i.e. the Teachers' Institute, Library of Parliament (CA) and the Citizenship Foundation, UK).

A careful process of selection and recruitment was established. Extensive pre-departure preparation was organized with inputs during five meetings at each site focusing on general cultural awareness, some limited linguistic preparation, insights into the nature of education systems and issues about citizenship education. The publication 'Ready, Steady, Go' (produced by Queen's University, Ontario) was used as a guide to the practical preparations needed for international travel. Dialogues were established between host and guest students prior to departure by means of e-mail. The partners agreed (individually and institutionally) that the work undertaken by students who would take part in exchanges would be recognized as part of their normal programme of study.

The students were also guided before departure to produce a piece of written work that would aid their understanding of citizenship and citizenship education. It was explained that the mobile students were expected to complete a 'Citizenship Education Learning File'.

This would include an investigatory project. It was agreed that in addition to a school placement for each student there would be a programme of activities that helped students to learn more about the host country, to experience general professional development and to understand more about citizenship education. This programme of activities varied according to local circumstances but an example can be given from Berlin. Guided visits often including a talk by an expert took place to the 'topography of terrors' (the ruins of the former headquarters of the German Gestapo); Checkpoint Charlie and museum; Berlin Parliament (local government); Reichstag (national government); Jewish Museum (including a talk on Holocaust education in Germany); Anne Frank Zentrum; House of the Wannsee Conference; Berlin Museum; Stasi prison; Sachenhausen Memorial site (former concentration camp). A seminar was held on the theme of citizenship education in Berlin and visits were made to four schools serving very different socio-economic and cultural areas.

The project was launched on both sides of the Atlantic by significant involvement in high profile conferences and a number of papers have already been published as a result of involvement with the project. When we invited feedback from mobile students we found that 97 per cent of the respondents awarded a grade of 4 or 5 (with 5 being the best and 1 the worst) about their overall reaction to the experience.

The evaluation of the project

A qualitative evaluation methodology was adopted, influenced by the 'illuminative evaluation' model developed by Parlett and Hamilton (1977) which aims:

> to discover and document what it is like to be participating in the scheme, whether as teacher or pupil; and, in addition, to discern and discuss the innovation's most significant features, recurring concomitants and critical processes. (p. 10)

A variety of data were collected including the individual written applications to take part, group conversations and individual feedback. Documentary analysis was undertaken in all three years of the project. Documents were exchanged between partners in order to develop initial understandings about the aims and processes of teacher education programmes in the countries involved in the project. We analysed the written descriptions of programmes established for those who became mobile as well as the written assignments produced by students. The students were asked to apply to become mobile and as such we had a written record of their expectations and their previous experiences that would help to place their subsequent reactions and achievements in context. While we would not claim that we had a very clear benchmark from which to assess the contribution made by the project, we would suggest that we had a form of awareness of students' backgrounds prior to their involvement in our project. During the period of mobility students were asked to write on three occasions (beginning, middle and end of their exchange) comments about their reactions to the experience. On each of those occasions students were asked to write about 500–1000 words in response to the questions shown below.

What do you expect to gain or face problems (or have gained/have faced problems) associated with:

(i) personal/individual hopes/concerns (money, accommodation, broader cultural horizons, etc.);
(ii) what do you expect to gain/face challenges (or have gained/ have faced problems) in a general professional sense (learning about systems in your host country);
(iii) what do you expect to gain/face challenges about (or have gained/have faced problems) in relation to citizenship education

   (a) what sort of model of citizenship education are you hoping to learn about – global education, moral education, political literacy, community involvement, etc.;
   (b) what sort of approach – whole school or classroom based;
   (c) what sort of focus – teaching, assessing, counselling).

(iv) any other comments?

At the end of an exchange each student completed an eight-page feedback form that included seven main sections: placement school; programme of additional activities; accommodation and catering; travel; budget; recommendation; preparation. There were twenty prompts across the seven categories for the students that were intended to allow for open, full and focused responses. There were opportunities for students to give a grade (one for the most negative reaction and five for the most positive reaction) in relation to three areas (school placement, accommodation and an overall judgement about the project).

A significant amount of data were collected through interviews. The three issues of personal, general professional development for teachers and citizenship education were used as a focus for the three extended written statements provided by students although care was taken to allow for other issues to be followed as directed by the respondent. All students were interviewed both individually and as a member of a group. Interviews were lead either by the member of staff who visited mobile students or a representative of the home institution.

The collection of data through informal methods also took place. Extensive e-mail correspondence between staff and students, and students and students provided a rich source by which issues came to the fore. It is not claimed that all correspondence was seen by the evaluators but rather that a significant amount of material was available for analysis. (Of course, students knew that an evaluation was taking place, which would lead to data being used, and were free to copy members of staff into the correspondence.) The issues that emerged from such correspondence and conversations with teachers and between members of the project team came to provide useful insights into what students were doing, what qualities in relation to their role as beginning teachers and citizenship educators were being displayed and what perceptions were being generated.

During analysis of the qualitative data we used a process of category generation and saturation derived from Glaser and Strauss (1967). This process has been used frequently by others (e.g. Vulliamy and Webb, 2003) and is appropriate for our approach to evaluation. Our interest in the issues of personal and professional development with a focus on citizenship education made us especially careful always to ensure an ethical approach to data collection and analysis. Four issues are particularly important. First, students knew that they were involved in a process of evaluation, were encouraged to share information and comments only when they felt it was appropriate to do so and were guaranteed anonymity. Secondly, we aimed to develop a collaborative approach to evaluation. All staff became involved in the agreed standard collection of data from students, and also in the provision of additional data if they felt that there were interesting probes and prompts that could be used. Discussions took place in various 'zones' (within Canada; within Europe; across the whole transatlantic team) that we hoped would allow for appropriate 'local' expertise to be deployed without losing a sense of overarching coherence. Thirdly, we wanted to avoid a situation in which in the process of evaluating our own work we would develop a comfortably positive analyses. While it was not possible for us to engage an external evaluator, we were careful to invite involvement and comment from beyond the central teams whenever possible. The encouragement of the writing of an MA dissertation (with the involvement of an external examiner), the contributions made by the associate partners who were essential and valued contributors, but perhaps not as central to the success of the project as the seven universities, and the writing of a number of pieces about the project (all of which were subject to peer review) make it possible to argue that our results have been subject to critical external judgement. Fourthly, we were aware of the complex and at times unhelpful relationships that have been established between project staff and funding agencies (e.g. Torrance, 2003). The points made above about the relationship we established with external reviewers are partly helpful in relation to this issue. However, we have deliberately built this negative possibility into our thinking and, as we are now beyond the funding point, we do not feel subject to any external influence and have not, in any case, felt subject to inappropriate suggestions about the ways in which the evaluation could develop.

Issues arising from data analysis

We will discuss a number of issues in four sections: logistics, personal enhancement, general professional development, citizenship education.

Logistics

The project demanded a very high input by all staff and students. The total amounts available from project funding did not recognize the full costs. Furthermore the unequal arrangements for funding (only 50 per cent for Europeans compared to 75 per cent for Canadians) were not helpful as we experienced unequal flows of mobile student teachers. A number of problematic issues emerged indirectly from this rather unsatisfactory financial context. Since the early 1990s in England, schools have been paid by universities to mentor students. Without payment schools do not normally accept students on teaching practice. Although schools that hosted students have been very under-standing and helpful, the need to explain to senior management teams that money could not be transferred in the usual way proved to be time-consuming and awkward.

In a complex programme involving nine institutions in four countries, some very challenging but 'normal' difficulties are to be expected. The difficulties, as shown in the quotation below from one of the tutors, were manageable:

> well, problems, they are to do with the logistics of the programmes. You know it's one of these programmes that when you write a proposal it all seems coherent on paper, it's a wonderful idea and there is no reason why it can't happen. When you actually begin to negotiate at the details in terms of how are the ... , when are the exchanges going to take place, how are the students going to be evaluated, how does it fit into their own programme requirements. When you begin to look at the details then obviously all kinds of problems arise. And we still have those problems, this is the first year that we have done this programme so hopefully the second year will be better. But I don't see those as major problems. They are in a sense inevitable in a project that brings together 7 universities in 4 different countries. And particularly with the teams that we have they are very creative, very tolerant, they want to find solutions to the problems, I don't see that as a major issue.

However, the emergence of severe acute respiratory syndrome (SARS) in 2003 was very challenging. A complicated set of arrangements for exchanges to Toronto were already in place before the World Health Organisation (WHO) made its announcements about travel to Toronto. Those careful arrangements were cancelled and then, at the last minute, put back into place. One member of staff in Sweden engaged in lengthy negotiations with schools and even allowed Canadian students to live in her own apartment when other options became difficult.

There were also issues that related more obviously and explicitly to notions of citizenship, identity and belonging. Students had to ensure that they knew during their period of travel that their status remained unchanged as a person registered at their home institution, that they complete their boarding card to show that they were visiting for the purposes of 'leisure' and not work (as the latter could be misinterpreted as relating to paid employment) and that they were merely visiting schools and other sites rather than working with young people. We found challenges associated with the reactions of immigration officials. It was always extremely difficult to achieve replies to queries made to embassies. There seemed to be unwillingness on the part of officials to answer questions that would have assisted us. When, however, advice was given, it seemed to require expensive, time-consuming, intrusive and unnecessary procedures. One institution, following advice given by the Canadian embassy and their own university, decided in the first year of exchanges to encourage students to undertake a medical examination. The experience of this procedure was such that it was not repeated during the following year. There does seem a sense in which debates over globalization are moving rather faster than the bureaucracy does or, perhaps the fear of bureaucracy, allows. These matters perhaps relate to all international educational work but could be seen to be particularly pertinent to our citizenship project. The challenge of developing internationally framed professional development within a bureaucracy that is nationally based is problematic. This seems especially pertinent to our work in the context of citizenship education. It seemed to us that the nation state is defining the sort of citizenship that is held at the very moment that our project aims for a broader frame of reference. While we do recognize the challenges posed by globalization and higher education (DEA, 2002) we sometimes felt that we were facing more traditional barriers.

'Personal' issues

A variety of 'personal' issues arose. The most concrete – and negative, for Canadians moving to Europe – of students' experiences related to accommodation. Learning about the standards of living experienced by others proved not always to be entirely comfortable. Language learning was an issue that was discussed. We recognized that there may be a series of practical ('survival') matters as well as issues relating to the development of wider cultural horizons. Generally, the Europeans for whom English was not the first language viewed the challenge of using English as a very positive opportunity afforded by the placement. The following are fairly typical responses:

> The language is no problem for me. I have practised my English lots before. (Swedish student)

> I benefited from the experience from the language point of view. Being in an English speaking community naturally builds confidence in one's own command of English and widens one's knowledge of the vocabulary and improves one's communication skills. (German student)

The reactions from the Canadians who travelled to Europe were usually very different. English is widely spoken in Sweden and, perhaps, slightly less commonly in Germany. But members of staff in both these countries were aware of the potential difficulties for those who spoke no foreign languages. A tutor from Germany commented:

> It has been known to us before that – with one exception – the Canadian students had no knowledge of German. That's why we were looking for what is called 'bilingual schools', the so called 'Europa-Schulen', which in some cases offer English as the second language (for sciences and social studies). These schools provide the chance to the Canadians to speak in their mother tongue which helps them to understand much more of what is going on in the actual school.

It was also possible to make use of one or two Canadian students who had family backgrounds that included some familiarity with a foreign language. All students were asked to undertake language preparation if they were going to a country where the first language was different from their own. But the extent to which this happened varied and it was unfortunate that feedback from students did not always reflect the responsibility that staff had encouraged them to take. In response to a question about language preparation the following can be seen as fairly typical from Canadian students going to Germany:

Minimal. Personal attempt at learning the language. (Berlitz method)

Totally inadequate. We all should have been given basic training before departure.

The German members of staff commented:

We strongly recommend that Canadian exchange students should have a basic course of German before they come to the country. Although there is no problem to converse in English in every day situation, it would deepen their understanding of the problems within German education with a basic knowledge of the German language. In this case it will be easy to identify papers, curriculum paragraphs, schoolbook sides etc. of interest which in such a case could be translated by members of the German buddy group, school students or teachers.

Although minimal preparation can work within Europe, in ERASMUS/ SOCRATES schemes that require a placement of anything up to one academic year the short placements of four to six weeks were inadequate for allowing for effective language learning. At times it felt to some as if we were caught between choosing students who already had appropriate language skills (with the potential drawback of not having a very significant impact upon certain individuals) and tailoring activities for the monolingual students with the possibility that some would have an unexceptional set of experiences during the placement.

Generally, and less tangibly than the specific 'personal' issues discussed above, there was an extremely positive reaction to taking part in an international placement. The typical response was, in the words of one European student, 'rewarding and inspiring'. A typical response from a Canadian student is shown below:

I gained a lot personally and I think that one thing came about from my own independent travel. I got to see a lot of different parts of the country and meet different people and talk to them. And I was blown away with the friendliness that I experienced. Especially when people found out that I was not American that I was Canadian, because I had a few snide comments made to me about being American.

What, then, did they find so rewarding? In the quotations above there is the sense of discovering a friendly and positive approach in a new environment. At times, specific benefits were highlighted. One German student, for example, suggested that:

> Being in North America was a very special feeling. I felt part of and close to the news and the international stage of world politics and its most dominating actors (and actresses). From that perspective 'German theatre' (i.e. home affairs) in contrast to the 'big stage' seemed rather tedious and of little relevance.

A Swede supported this feeling: 'When being at home in Sweden it feels small and I just want to go into the big world again.' An English student commented that to visit a country in which bilingualism and issues relating to first nation culture were readily discussed was a great opportunity. One student from Berlin said 'first of all' we 'learned about other customs, laws and cultural diversity living together in peace'. A Canadian commented:

> the experience has had a great impact on me personally and professionally. It has broadened my knowledge in citizenship education, curriculum development, instructional strategies and teaching across the curricula. It has provided me with a greater interest into the subject of citizenship education as an area for further research that I intend to pursue in the future. It has given me a greater understanding of global education and the importance of having a global perspective in teaching citizenship education.

These very positive reactions about the general experience of coming to terms with another culture and the opportunity to discover more about specific cultural and political issues did much, as students wrote and said explicitly, to develop confidence and self-esteem. A European student said: 'My self confidence increased and I lived in a foreign country by myself and very soon it was home.' There was a sense in which these comments demonstrated the power of the experience to take them beyond stereotypes.

> In the context of this project I was able to travel and visit schools and historical sites in Sweden, Germany and England. My direct involvement in the project

caused me to re-think my cultural constructions course in terms of its overlap with the subject of social studies in general and notions of citizenship in particular.

There are many things that one learns from this experience. Probably the most significant learning for me was the opportunity to meet instructors from the various universities involved in the project and to discuss with them ideas about their education systems and citizenship education in particular. It also deepened my understandings of the benefits and complexities involved in working collaboratively on international projects of this type.

It seems that there are many opportunities to learn about one's own country as one moves, geographically, away from it but psychologically closer to it. One of the Swedish students commented:

Whenever I have travelled somewhere the Swedish side of me comes out and I become more proud of my country. When I am at home I don't think of how I act that much, it's an everyday life. But when you get somewhere else in the world you automatically start to think of how you do things at home. And I often see all the good sides of Sweden and I get more proud. I feel more national when I am in another country but once I am back in Sweden I feel more global because of all the places I have visited and all the experience I have got.

A German student commented:

From the distance of thousands of kilometres we also learned a lot about our home country. We understand some things better now because we are sensitised for a different view and have a better awareness of this now.

The Canadians reflected the same perspective. One Canadian student observed:

it gave me a renewed appreciation for Canadian multiculturalism – especially in Toronto . . . I think the level and respect for diversity and multiculturalism significantly affects one's approach to citizenship.

A final issue to be explored in the context of 'personal' issues relates to a potential tension within the project. Given our interests in a democratic form of citizenship education, we discussed the appropriateness of providing what could be perceived as a luxury experience for already well-travelled high status adults. We wished to promote equal opportunities in higher education (especially those that relate to gender, social class and 'race', e.g. Kerckhoff, Fogelman and Manlove [1997] and Morgan [1996]) and wanted to work against the possibility of some who are perhaps too ready to 'know their limits' (see Gayle, Berridge and Davies, 2002; Archer and Yamashita, 2003; Forsyth and Furlong, 2003). To this end we included a range of students from East as well as West Berlin, women as well as men and those with so-called non-traditional backgrounds. We expected that only those students who did not have additional responsibilities would be able to become mobile (Reay, Ball and David, 2002), although we were pleasantly surprised to be proved wrong on occasion. We also worried that we would add to students' difficulties at a time when debt is common for those in higher education (Clare, 2003). We wanted to assist the process of widening access (Alexiadou, 2002; Canning, 2003) without contributing to a process that would negatively assist the further establishment of markets in higher education (Dill, 2003; Jongbloed, 2003). It is true that some of our mobile students had extensive international experience and some even had family in their host country. But most had not been outside Europe or North America prior to their experience in the project and there were examples of students who went on a plane for the first time in order to undertake their exchange.

Of course, ultimately, we were unsure as to the future impact that the project would have on the mobile students. Were we in the business of helping to create opinion formers who would lead others towards the benefits of international co-operation or was their placement an opportunity for 'ordinary' people to experience those benefits at first hand? For the most part we were content to look for the positive and, while not constructing artificial barriers, we were concerned to act in a way that would have maximum impact. One tutor commented:

> I think there is enormous potential in these exchanges. It depends to some extent upon the students, I think it's a larger impact probably on those who haven't travelled much and haven't experienced other cultures and for them it can be a life changing a life enhancing experience.

General professional development

There are some strong views put forward by students. It was common for both Canadians and Europeans to see their own experiences at home as being far more stressful than those which affected people elsewhere. School experience played a significant part of their placements and students from England, for example, could not believe that Canadian students were relatively untroubled by curriculum frameworks and testing and that teachers were not inspected. Comments about staff rooms often included the word 'relaxed' with suggestions that there were many more leisure related conversations than they were used to. One student went so far as to write:

> Schools in [place] seem to be 20 possibly 30 years behind developments in Britain. In many respects they are in need of a radical shake up. There is nothing in the curriculum that says that teachers should teach in the fashion that they do. [place] is arguably in need of a national curriculum or uniform guide that teachers' must adhere to and probably school inspectors to make sure that such a system is being adhered to.

This perhaps suggests that some students have already come to appreciate, to a greater extent, the philosophical approaches and practical applications of their own system and that they may be unable to fully appreciate approaches and applications that exist beyond their own contexts.

Some of the Canadians were surprised at the seemingly relaxed nature of European life. Some suggested that the pressurized existence that they were used to at home did not exist. Instead they noted teachers having regular and frequent breaks and adhering to standard ways of doing things that meant not staying after school when the occasion demanded. One – admittedly unusually strong – example of a student who held to that perception seemed to suggest that the host teachers would benefit from the student teachers' experience as shown below:

> The skills we had to offer in schools were underused. They didn't know what they could get from us. I felt I was very prepared and what I prepared wasn't used. . . . Initially we were just observing and then when they found out what we are capable of doing they tapped into that.

The Canadian students in England had to adapt quickly to a system that, very unlike their own, is driven by the existence of a National Curriculum and national inspection agency. While new knowledge was acquired, certain misunderstandings were evident as outlined in the quotation shown below:

> One of the differences would be that they have a National Curriculum but they actually have a book full of lesson plans in their entirety with the supporting pages and handouts and the equipment needed and the material needed to teach their lesson at their finger tips. So in Canada we would have to assemble all the material ourselves and in England they don't.

It appears that she believes, inaccurately, that the National Curriculum is in force in the United Kingdom, that there is very tight central control over the fine detail of what is taught in the classroom and that teachers do not write their own curriculum materials.

Perhaps unsurprisingly, the students made a number of rather sweeping generalizations as a result of their school experiences. Many Canadian and Europeans, however, seemed to develop a common notion of two issues. They quickly came to claim that the Canadian school students were academically less pressured but socially more mature. This inverse relationship between ability and relationships was raised frequently. One comment from a Canadian student teacher about students in English schools is typical:

> I've probably seen 12 different classes and most of them have been the same. I really feel the students here surpass my students in Canada for educational ability. They can quickly get to work at times, they know how to write an essay, they know how to study, they know how to do some of those organizational things, but they don't really know how to behave.

Many of the Canadian students were quite shocked at the nature of the relationships between teachers and students in English classrooms. One student provided a stark example:

> Yesterday I witnessed something really distressing. If I were the girl I would be crying. They have uniforms. Shoes without platforms. You know these girls they are coming into womanhood. We're going on a field trip to

[a Church]. The students were told they had to wear flat shoes. They were told that in a letter. The girl with the shoes... I felt it was taken too far. 'You are just a stupid girl for wearing those shoes'. That would be completely unacceptable [in Canada]. Another example, students had to draw... some pupils did the whole page so she yelled at them. 'You deserve to get a detention'. She was so angry about her lesson being off. She threatened them with a detention. A girl got a detention because she didn't bring her pencil crayons. I saw things like that. It's a little bit of an eye opener.

One Canadian student commented succinctly and drily:

you [i.e. teachers in England] are way more straightforward with your children. Shut up and sit down! Well!

Students were able to apply these insights to citizenship education:

On a number of occasions in the course of my study of citizenship education I found myself wondering if it could be possible that the people involved truly understood the implications of what they were saying for education and society. As teachers, we must surely be aware that it makes little pedagogical sense to attempt to teach students about participatory democracy from within a system of education that is strongly hierarchical in structure, not particularly inclusive, and regulated with powerful social control mechanisms. I think that Professor Crick is quite right that citizenship education can and should be a profoundly transformative activity.

Another commented:

I have concluded that the essential challenge in providing effective citizenship education is not about curriculum and course work, but rather about making a true commitment to democratic processes and a definition of citizenship on a global scale.

Such propositions are helpful but not necessarily because they suggest some sort of 'truth' has been discovered. Rather, there is very clear evidence of students trying to make sense of their own experience. They make mistakes and say and write things that are often simply inaccurate or insensitively controversial, but they are engaging in a real and very challenging professional development exercise. It seemed clear from various statements that they made and the lively way in which they made them that they had never before been challenged in such a fundamental manner. As such, we are not arguing that these examples of strongly held views and, at times, misperceptions are necessarily negative outcomes. As one fairly representative student remarked in her evaluation: 'I think I will realize more when I get into my own classroom how much I learned.' It may be helpful in future initiatives of this type for tutors to provide more formal attention to learning activities such as seminars or additional readings that would assist mobile students to better contextualize their observations.

Citizenship education

Prior to their exchange some students imagined that the people on the opposite side of the Atlantic are more knowledgeable and have more expertise to develop citizenship education. In England, for example, the very recent introduction of citizenship education into the National Curriculum heightened students' interest. One European student commented:

> citizenship in England is relatively in its infancy and so the opportunity to see citizenship in action in a context where it is more established will be invaluable.

But citizenship is relatively new elsewhere (at times the term 'citizenship education' is not used at all) and a Canadian student spoke for many when she suggested that 'answers' could be found away from her home country:

> There is no compulsory citizenship education in my home province . . . I am hoping that the actual defining of citizenship movements going on in the UK will help me as a citizenship educator.

Interestingly, however, some of that citizenship education occurred not through any organized programme but rather through the experience of being abroad and of making arrangements to go abroad. We have already referred above to the challenges associated with immigration.

In such contexts the goal of global citizenship contrasted sharply with the experience of nationally oriented officials who seemed to be either unhelpful in their passivity concerning the provision of information or inappropriately assertive. Once their placements had begun, students had an opportunity to see at first hand the reaction to extremely controversial political issues in another country. The exchanges in 2003 took place immediately prior to the war in Iraq. The war was obviously a very significant feature of media reports. The opportunity to see not only how another country reacted to these events but also to see how one's own country was portrayed by others was keenly felt. This issue also impacted directly on school life with, for example, leaflets being distributed about a motion drafted and passed by the Trustees of the Toronto District School Board relating to the ways in which controversial issues could be discussed and inviting action by teachers and others. Issues of citizenship were thrown into stark relief. Students were very affected by these issues with assignments being written on the ways in which controversial issues were and could be discussed.

Students found it stimulating to be taken out of their own environment and placed into a very different setting. The issue of multiculturalism and multicultural education was very obviously a key issue for many of the students. Some of the Europeans remarked very positively on the multicultural nature of some schools in Toronto. The opportunity to see teachers creating simulations in which immigrants had to be attracted to a country was a welcome change of emphasis for some Europeans. It was a curious experience for some of the students from Toronto to be taken from this multicultural context and placed by project staff, who were keen to develop pluralistic understandings, into an environment where as one student remarked, '[name of school] is about as un-multicultural as they come'. An interesting twist in experiences with multiculturalism was the two New Brunswick students who were placed in [name of school] in London. For them this was a real experience with diversity as they come from a relatively monocultural part of Canada and this school's population is 100 per cent Bangladeshi Muslims. Both students, however, commented on the cultural isolation of the school and the lack of interest of the students to learn about other cultures. One wrote, 'The students at [name of school] are almost 100% Muslim-Bangladeshi, with many students interacting only in this culture both within and outside of school'. Another interesting situation was the English students who noted that their host school which included a large French Immersion programme and a stated commitment to teaching second language gave no indication of that in the public spaces: bulletin boards, entry ways, etc., where everything was in English. They pointed out that schools in England, at least in London, went out of their way to recognize diversity in language in these kinds of public spaces but did not teach the languages in the classroom. Perhaps in practice the project was helping to develop a sense of multiculturalism in national contexts as opposed to an untrammelled internationalism. For European students who had come from a community that was relatively restricted in its diversity, it was inspiring to be able to listen to university-based lectures in Canada about 'how to teach in a cultural context' and to visit a 'Native Elementary School'. It was fascinating for them 'to see the Maliseet language and culture being preserved in a westernised setting' even though 'it was clear that this was a relatively new and uncertain harmony'.

Of course, multicultural education is relevant to all students whatever their local circumstances but a challenge was perceived by some students as they moved across contexts. The nature of these challenges was at times surprising to students. Perhaps the starkest illustration of that surprise related to the different sense of nationality that was perceived. Student teachers from a relatively monocultural local context within Europe were very surprised by the singing of the Canadian national anthem in schools at the beginning of each day. The European (especially English) awareness of the evils of imperialism had perhaps led them to expect simple and inappropriate associations between national anthems and national identity. It was refreshing for them to question the extent to which patriotism could be distinguished from nationalism and to consider whether assimilation, multiculturalism or interculturalism was being practised. It was of great interest to see the extent to which English naturalization procedures are developing in a way that follows the Canadian model (Dyer, 2003; Travis, 2003). The UPEI students had a fascinating debate in Berlin about their being 'proud to be Canadian'. Their German counterparts said they would never claim to be 'proud to be German' due to their perceptions of its fascist overtones. It led to self-revelatory moments for the Canadians on the nature of patriotism and how cultures express it differently.

Involvement in school programmes helped students to explore these issues further. Those students (especially those from Germany) who had expressed an interest in Holocaust education were able to continue to develop their understanding in Canada. The interlocking histories of the nations represented in our project were explored, most notably by those who became involved in site visits. One Canadian student had the good fortune to be invited to accompany students on the school field trip to the World War One battlefields. She writes about the excitement she felt as they approached battlefields upon which Canadian troops had fought. After visiting Vimy Ridge, she commented:

> As we walked around the trenches and the memorial, several people gathered around me to share in my reactions. I have never been so proud to be Canadian. One of the teachers put out the question as to why Colonials seemed to be sent out on the more dangerous missions, rather than British troops. Some students correctly guessed that they were deemed more expendable. There was a true community of learning taking place in that scarred and pitted landscape.

Students also commented on their introduction to a number of extra-school organizations directly involved in citizenship education. Many were very impressed with organizations like the Citizenship Foundation in London and War Child Canada in Toronto. This kind of connection, between schools and NGOs, was one that some students felt brought more attention to the role of civil society in citizenship education and ought to be infused more explicitly.

The very broad interpretation of citizenship education could be problematic (Sears, 1996). A narrower (or some would say more focused) version of citizenship education might require a more explicit identification of political concepts that would provide a context within which students could learn and practise. In the light of the precision that is deemed to be necessary for teaching and learning models in higher education (e.g. see Duff, 2003) there may be a need for some greater clarity. Some have argued that staff may need a good deal of support before there is clear evidence of reliable assessment practices (e.g. Holroyd, 2000; Yorke, Bridges and Woolf, 2000). However, other responses need to be explored for the purposes of questioning the nature of the understanding that the students have achieved. We did not want to develop a form of understanding of students' progress that would emerge only from a bureaucratic approach that is closely related to mechanistic processes of assessment (Goodlad, 1999; Arjen and Jickling, 2003). One student who seemed to us to state the argument against formal and unhelpful assessment, commented:

> I have concluded that the essential challenge in providing effective citizenship education is not about curriculum and course work, but rather about making a true commitment to democratic processes and a definition of citizenship on a global scale.

While we came to accept the notion of characterising citizenship broadly, we do need to explore two related issues. Firstly, students' thinking about citizenship shifted at times without any real sense of coherence. Of course, we could argue more positively that students were being allowed to explore different notions of citizenship without being led dogmatically to one predetermined model but we are only prepared to go so far towards that position. The following quotation from a student shows perhaps the strengths and weaknesses of this loosely focused approach, revealing as it does the struggle for meaning that is ongoing (see Ofsted, 2003 for a more broadly based account of some of these challenging issues):

> I was thinking its [i.e. citizenship education] is about how to vote, everything that makes you a god citizen, all about how you make friends with people all the aspects of citizenship education. I was talking to the lady who did citizenship education [in the placement school] and she was talking about smoking, sunburn, you tell people to use sun lotion. I was so surprised, it was friendship and another theme and loneliness and air pollution. So I have been doing some research, looking for articles for her. So I was a bit surprised about sun-screen and about pollution.

Some greater clarity is needed for this student for her to be able to make sense of these sorts of shifts.

Secondly, in a broad characterization of citizenship we feel that the relative significance of classroom or school ethos is heightened. There were some extremely positive results of this approach. Students from Canada, for example, wrote intelligently and insightfully about the work of (name of school) in Sweden where democratic practices are observed. The student wrote about the very liberal atmosphere within the school in which rules are not imposed and drew attention to very positive work with asylum seekers. This, wrote the students, provided 'the experience of a lifetime'. However, the comments made about the atmosphere in English schools (quoted above) left some Canadian students with different impressions. Some of the English students were concerned that in some Canadian schools they 'observed lessons where over one third of the students are not engaged in the lesson. They are either listening to their headphones, asleep or feigning sleep.' The criticisms of a more relaxed social approach left some feeling uncomfortable:

> I have found the students are much more aware of topics such as tolerance, respect and discrimination than are their British counterparts. They have a very strong sense of right and wrong which is what I believe contributes to their generally respectful attitude towards each other. However, it can also be limiting as they find it hard to think outside narrow concepts of 'good' and 'bad'. In one class I observed on the Russian revolution a student asked who the good guys were between the Bolsheviks and Mensheviks. In addition the students are not given the opportunity to question or to think round topics as much as they are in Britain although they are perfectly capable of this when encouraged. Teaching seems to take a consensus approach to history and be delivered in the style of lectures and copying notes. I have also found it strange to work without schemes of work or any form of public exam system. Whether a student 'passes' a course at the end of a semester depends wholly on the discretion of the teacher.

We do not have answers to these challenging issues but feel that the project has allowed a useful, professional exploration. We do not claim that this is necessarily different from work in other areas (e.g. debates about the nature of history are represented in classic and recent titles such as Carr, 1975; Jenkins, 1991; Lemon, 1995). It seems, however, that there would be some value in exploring further what would be regarded as the broad parameters of citizenship education if we were to be able to debate within an area as opposed to the possibility of discussing issues that are potentially different in type. Without some clarity about meaning there could be a risk of academic incoherence, misunderstandings on the part of applicants to degree programmes and low status.

Conclusions

The 'Promoting Citizenship Education through Initial Teacher Education' project has been an exhausting and challenging process. We have succeeded in moving students and staff across the Atlantic in a way that allows them, generally, to grow personally as well as in terms of professional development and in relation to citizenship education. We are convinced that the experience of the project will be of great benefit to all participants. One Canadian student, not used to travelling on her own, expressed this positive outcome succinctly:

Personally, this experience has allowed me to see, think and feel differently. I've grown with this experience, since I'd to make my own decisions and know what will work best in certain situations.

Chapter 10

Textual apologism or dissent?
Ethical dilemmas for academics in managerialist times

Martin Thrupp

Whether to serve the existing political order or act as 'critic and conscience' has often been an important ethical dilemma for academics working in higher education. Nevertheless this ethical burden is not shared equally over time or across higher education. Over some historical periods government policy is especially unjust and some areas of study are potentially more closely aligned with government policy than others. When academics are working both in an era of problematic government policies and in a relatively 'applied' area with potentially close application to those policies, their work in higher education will pose especially acute ethical dilemmas.

In the present managerialist times, management as a field of study in higher education is firmly in the ethical hot seat. Management has come to be seen as *the* solution to policy problems in many countries and yet there is also much evidence that the managerialist (and market and performative) approaches favoured are harmful. Consequently, management academics face a stark but usually unacknowledged ethical choice: should they promote such reforms or contest them?

This chapter considers how this problem plays out amongst academics working in higher education who teach and research about school management and leadership in England. As necessary background to the ethical dilemmas they face, I begin by briefly summarizing the case against the 'post-welfarist' school reforms in England since 1988 and then draw on a recent critical review of school management texts (Thrupp and Wilmott, 2003) to note the varying ways and extents to academics in the area of school management and leadership support or contest these reforms. On the basis of this review I argue that school management and leadership provides an example of an area where academics in higher education are ethically compromised by their support of government policy (albeit to importantly varying extents) and note that pressures in higher education may account for much of this problem.

Post-welfarist school reform

In much the same way as Tomlinson (2001) writes about *Education in a Post-Welfare Society* and Gewirtz (2002) discusses the 'post welfarist education policy complex', here the phrase 'postwelfarist school reform' is used as a kind of shorthand for the market, managerial, performative and prescriptive schooling policies and practices of the last fifteen years. Open Enrolment and Local Management of Schools introduced by the Conservatives under the 1988 Education Act were key planks of policy to create market competition amongst schools in England as were OfSTED inspections, introduced in 1992. When New Labour was elected in 1997 it retained these key market policies and has subsequently introduced what Hatcher (1998) has referred to as 'Official School Improvement' (OSI). This involves numerous new managerial and performative initiatives intended to further raise academic standards and improve national economic competitiveness. These have included target-setting, the promotion of a bidding culture (honey-pot management), Performance Related Pay, the Literacy and Numeracy Strategies, Specialist Schools and City Academies. Reinforcing these developments, New Labour has also promoted what Ozga (2000) has called 'Official School Leadership' (OSL) through the National College of School Leadership (NCSL). The role of the NCSL is to relay New Labour's education policy programme into schools through a series of 'designer leadership' courses (Gronn, 2003). For intending headteachers in England the courses are difficult to evade, indeed the best known one, the National Professional Qualification for Headteachers (NPQH), has become mandatory in 2004.

Were they more clearly benign, neither OSI nor OSL would pose much of an ethical dilemma for academics working in higher education in the area of school management and leadership. However, it is increasingly apparent that the policies promoted by New Labour do have many harmful effects. Research suggests that the main problems include increasingly polarized schools and communities, a narrowed educational focus in schools and the loss of authenticity in the teaching and learning process, a reduction in the sociability of schools and communities, the commodification and marginalization of children, the distraction of existing teachers and school leaders from educational matters, the discouragement of potential teachers and school leaders and the undermining of more progressive policies. On the other hand some of the claimed benefits of the new order like greater autonomy for schools, reduced student and school failure, better employment prospects and reduced social exclusion are often overplayed because there is a considerable mismatch between the rhetoric and what seems to be really going on (e.g. Gillborn and Youdell, 2000; Gleeson and Husbands, 2001; Gewirtz, 2002; see also Thrupp and Wilmott, 2003).

Textual apologism and dissent

If one accepts such research evidence on the limitations of post-welfarist school reform, or even some of it, supporting the thrust of current education policy in England becomes ethically problematic for those in higher education teaching and writing about school management and leadership. Yet on the whole, such limitations are being highlighted by policy sociologists rather than education management academics. To find out how education management academics deal with the politics of education, Rob Wilmott and I recently undertook a review of education management texts written since 1995: *Education Management in Mangerialist Times* (Thrupp and Wilmott, 2003). This review pointed to four broad political stances amongst education management writers: primarily problem-solving texts, overt apologism, subtle apologism and textual dissent. It should be noted that these categories are extremely broad and not in any sense rigidly bounded or intended to portray perspectives which are fixed or static.[1] Rather they are intended to provide a way of getting some purchase on the educational management literature but they need to be informed by specific arguments about particular writers.

Primarily problem-solving texts

There are innumerable primarily problem-solving education management and leadership texts but they are more often written by practitioners and consultants than 'serious' education management academics. The key point about these texts is that you would barely know from them that schooling occurs in the context of education reform or structural inequality. In this sense these texts are 'apolitical' but then avoiding a concern with politics is itself a highly political position, one which fits easily within a technicist and managerialist approach.

An example is Horne and Brown's (1997) *500 Tips for School Improvement*. This book contains 48 sections generally providing 10 short tips, most of which are socially and politically decontextualized. This is unsurprising since the 'tips' format required by books in this series undoubtedly precludes any more complex discussion of the problems and possibilities of school improvement. When the tips do raise features of post-welfarist school reform or refer to DfES and OfSTED sources and advice, this is usually done in an uncritical, taken-for-granted, manner. This is true even when there is (rare) acknowledgement of debate:

> 8. Try the Competency approach [to appraisal]. This may be an emotive subject. But the Teacher Training Agency (TTA) has guidelines for training

---

1. Within the same category are writers with somewhat varying perspectives and writers may often write differently for different audiences or move between perspectives even for the same audience, or just write in equivocal ways which are hard to pin down. Individual outlooks can also change markedly, perhaps as a result of some incident which prompts a rethink or sometimes just a dawning realization that something different needs to be done.

new teachers using competence-based appraisal. We assess pupils by giving clear criteria. So why not assess teachers in a similar way?

(Horne and Brown, 1997: 111)

Overt apologism

Our review found relatively few texts which were examples of overt apologism. These bring post-welfarist school reform into the frame more but their stance is uncritically supportive and they barely acknowledge the social justice concerns associated with it. For overt apologists the problem is generally how to restructure the school so that it fits with the ideologies and technologies of neo-liberal and managerial reform, it is certainly not how to contest that reform. A good example is provided by the first (long) paragraph in Davies and Ellison's (1997) book *School Leadership for the 21st Century*. Consider both the language and the substantive argument:

> It is our contention that there are two waves of reform that occur in education systems. The first is the changes to the structure and framework of the system. In the case of the UK, the National Curriculum, national testing and examination frameworks and school-based financial management allied to parental choice and new inspection and reporting systems can be seen to have been a radical reform and restructuring of the education system. The effectiveness of such reforms is of course partly determined by the nature of the reforms themselves and their implementation strategy but also in our view by the effectiveness of the second wave of the reform movement. This consists of the changes in the leadership and management behaviour of the individuals who are leading and managing the individual schools themselves. Just as the old saying 'you can take a horse to water but you cannot make it drink' is true, so giving individual leaders and managers in schools new responsibilities and accountability relationships does not, in itself, make them innovative and educationally entrepreneurial when their previous experience was in directive risk-adverse bureaucratic structures. The key to full realisation of effective schooling in a reformed and restructured education system depends on the capability of the leaders and the staff at the school level. We contend that having a clear understanding of the changing context in which education is now operating and of the constantly changing nature of selfmanaging schools, allied to a clear understanding by the educational leader of her/his own leadership and management skills to operate effectively in that environment, are prerequisites to undertaking successfully the key task

in leading and managing a school. *These understandings and skills enable the second round of reform at school level, that of creating effective schools in this new environment, to take place. These leadership and management perspectives form the central thrust of this book* ...

(Davies and Ellison, 1997: 1–2, my emphasis)

Davies' argument here may be summarized along the following lines: 'The main problem with the neo-liberal reform of educational structures is that they do not necessarily lead to changes in the hearts and minds of school leaders who cling to outdated ideas. As supporters of these reforms, we are trying to deal with this unfinished business of market and managerial colonization and this book is part of the process.' If left in any doubt, the reader is told that the book is 'of particular value to those on the Teacher Training Agency's programmes for headteacher development as it combines a similar competency and content approach' (p. 2). Ironically, critical empirical research which has explored the extent to which the reforms after 1988 have colonized the perspectives and practices of school leaders (e.g. Bowe, Ball and Gold, 1992) is not mentioned. Presumably this is because this kind of literature is much less convinced that turning out 'educationally entrepreneurial' school leaders is a good thing. The rest of the book is also all about how to be a smart school leader within a managerialist framework (see Thrupp and Wilmott, 2003: 147–152).

Subtle apologism

The majority of education management and leadership texts we reviewed in *Education Management in Mangerialist Times* had more discussion of post-welfarist school reform than primarily problem-solving texts but were less upbeat than overtly apologist ones. Rather they were cases of subtle apologism which indicate some concern about markets, managerialism and performativity in education but provide support for it either because their dissenting element is not emphasized enough within their *overall* account to provide any serious challenge or because their critique is insufficiently critical.

Precisely because the apologism is subtle, it is hard to give concise examples (see Thrupp and Wilmott, 2003, Chs 5–9 for detailed examples) but the first kind of problem mentioned above is illustrated fairly briefly in *Effective School Leadership* (MacBeath, 1998a). This book displays some awareness of the limitations of recent education reform, but offers strangely mixed messages not just because it is an edited collection. This book, based on an international study of school leaders in England, Denmark, Scotland and Australia, begins by noting that all were experiencing devolution, accountability, performativity and marketization. The book is positioned by discussing a series of questions which guided the study but there is an ambiguity here about whether it was intended to provide a critique of post-welfarist education reform or a guide to 'boxing clever' within it:

> These [reforms] brought new pressures and with them, changing expectations of schools and school leadership. For people in positions of leadership it posed the question 'whose expectations count and how should differing or conflicting expectations be resolved?' We wondered how headteachers, faced with the growing tensions of management and leadership, were able to reconcile the conflicting demands on them. Were some better than others? If so what was their secret and where had they learned it?
>
> (Kruchov, MacBeath and Riley, 1998: xii)

Further into the book there seems to be some support for managerialist reform:

> principals must address their attitudes to change and futures orientation. Principals have no way of making their schools immune from the influences of governments, educational policymakers and members of the wider world of business, industry and commerce...Principals' learning must embrace the vision and values inherent in innovation and the requirements of mandated change.
>
> (Dempster and Logan, 1998: 96)

However, there is also some constrained but clear critique of the direction of reform, especially in a chapter on 'ethical challenges in school leadership':

> On the one hand there are those who are pushing schools to operate like businesses and to pursue the educational equivalent of profit maximisation. On the other hand schools are ultimately concerned with the development of students who are not only employable, but also autonomous, responsible,

moral individuals who are effective members of society. . . . Heads who are able to model moral leadership in the way they run their schools are more likely, in our view, to concentrate on the ultimate goal of schooling, even though they are constantly under pressure to do otherwise.

(Dempster and Mahony, 1998: 137–138).

But most of the time the discussion is more ambiguous than either of these. For instance, this chapter ending:

We can also see how reforms may begin to modify behaviour by accentuating certain aspects of the job and downgrading others and where some of the resultant discomfort for school leaders may arise as they feel themselves pulled away from what they regard as effective practice towards new models dictated from the centre.

(Reeves, Moos and Forrest, 1998: 58)

Further confusing matters are contributions which do not relate clearly to the aim of the study, for instance MacBeath's opening chapter on 'Seven selected heresies of leadership' (MacBeath, 1998b). The problem with this book then is not that it does not offer a critical perspective but rather that other readings are more likely because of the way the book is written.

In an otherwise excellent account of school improvement, Gray's (2001) discussion of 'Special Measures', part of the OSI regime in the England, provides a concise example of the second kind of problem, critique which is insufficiently critical. Here Gray comments:

[t]he case of so-called 'failing' schools in England, however, presents a situation where questions about the speed and extent of improvement have become crucial to schools' survival. These schools have typically been given only a two year window to secure a turnaround. (p. 16)

Although one senses that Gray thinks this is problematic, he provides no discussion of the rights or wrongs of the policy. Similarly he goes on to raise questions about the supposed success of Special Measures but only in the most gentle way. Instead of saying that firm evidence for the success of Special Measures is just not there, particularly given OfSTED's weak inspection methodology and highly politicized stance, he uses phrases such as 'Unfortunately, whilst inspectors have doubt-lessly been able to convince themselves that changes have occurred in specific cases, more systematic evidence [on improvement in achievement] across large numbers of schools has yet to be published' (p. 17) and '…evidence on what it is [about improved "capacities"] which has actually impressed inspectors is harder to come by' (p. 18).

Textual dissent

Our review found dissenting texts few in number, and in fact more often written by policy sociologists with an interest in education management and leadership (e.g. Ball, 1994; Grace, 1995; Blackmore, 1999) than by education management specialists themselves.[2] Textual dissenters either challenge the textual apologists above directly by critique of textual apologism or more indirectly by providing an alternative account. However the key point about textually dissenting accounts is that one is left in no doubt that the authors are concerned about challenging post-welfarist school reform.

For instance, *Troubling Women* (Blackmore, 1999) is particularly concerned with feminist leadership and the way it is placed at risk in managerialist times. Blackmore points out that while feminists find post-modern discourses of education self-governance seductive because the local is thought to be more democratic, in reality women's experiences of selfmanaging leadership is very modernist – controlling and conforming. While this may be the case for both men and women, women find this 'doubly difficult' since they are overseeing the feminization, casualization and deprofessionalization of teaching, are more likely to be located in poor, multicultural 'failing' schools, and have to perform 'strong leadership' and 'managed change' roles which are hostile to their preferred mode of collegiality and genuine debate (p. 156). Blackmore also illustrates how women leaders end up doing a lot of what she calls 'emotional management', where they are supposed to 'manage' productively for the school the unpro-ductive emotions of anger, disillusionment and alienation amongst students, teachers and themselves (see pp. 162–165). Essentially, then,

---

2. Gunter (2001) is one important exception. Most dissenting texts are in leadership where there is a raft of what Grace (2000) calls 'critical leadership studies'.

Blackmore offers an account of feminist leadership in managerialist times which fundamentally unsettles uncritical and problem-solving accounts of leadership. The 'greedy organizations' of the post-welfarist era have a negative impact on those who work in them, especially women, that is not adequately acknowledged for instance in the literature around transformational leadership. Blackmore ultimately comes back to the question of whether we really want leadership, even if reconstituted. Indeed she is really inviting readers to join a critically informed feminist *educational* project rather than a leadership one.

Why few dissenting accounts of school management and leadership?

There appears to be two interrelated reasons why academics working in higher education are not writing more dissenting accounts of school leadership and management. One is the limited theoretical and epistemological roots of the education management field. Although there are texts like *Theories of Educational Management* (Bush, 2003), education management has generally favoured relatively weak forms of organizational rather than social theory despite schools being inherently social places. This lack of a socially theoretical orientation to issues of power and politics has often left education management writers poorly prepared to explore the limitations of OSI or OSL. As Fitz (1999: 318) has put the problem:

> EMS [education management studies] looks like a field without an 'ology', that is, many studies are not intellectually underpinned by explicit social theory. Thus it is difficult to see that 'management' is about relative distributions of power and authority and that there are fundamental questions about who holds legitimate authority (and on what basis), if you haven't read your Lukes, Foucault, Weber, Durkheim, Marx, Talcott Parsons, Bernstein, Bourdieu or Giddens, to name just a few.

Moreover as demonstrated by Wilmott (1999) writing about school effectiveness research, the epistemological commitments of education management and leadership writers will often not allow them to recognize how their work is problematic to textual dissenters:

> Their commitment to a positivist epistemology... itself causally conditions
> their indignant response [to external critics]... exponents of school effective-
> ness are unable to see the full force of the criticisms levelled against them
> since the causal mechanisms postulated by critics... are deemed to have no
> real existence and thus are held not to be permissible contenders in their
> explanatory framework.
>
> (Wilmott, 1999: 255)

Whereas the realist perspectives favoured by textual dissenters tend
to see schooling problems rooted in inegalitarian social structures,
the positivist epistemology favoured by most education management
writers reduces social structures to atomized individuals and schools
in a way which disavows structural inequality. In short, education
management apologists and dissenters may be often coming from
such different epistemological (and hence theoretical premises) that
textual apologists may not even be particularly interested in the
critical concerns of dissenters. Instead they will exhibit what one
critic of school effectiveness research has described as a 'distressing
blindness to the ideologically and epistemologically situated nature
of [their] own intellectual position' (Fielding, 1997: 139).

However theoretical allegiance is not the only, or even the most
important, reason for the lack of dissent in the school management
and leadership arena. Another key issue is the entrepreneurial and
problem-solving nature of the field, with this in turn related to the
relatively immediate relationship between school management and
leadership academics and the needs of practitioners. As Fitz (1999: 315)
also points out, education management discourse is located

> in a material base in which knowledge has a generally recognised exchange
> value. In this field, for example, it is not unusual for relations between field
> occupants to involve a cash nexus. Indeed... academics and entrepreneurs
> are expected and/or required to offer practitioners 'practical' guidance on
> how to make their institutions more effective and productive. This advice is
> in turn, taken as evidence of their utility and expertise.

Consequently there is much pressure for the accounts of school
management and leadership writers to be 'useful' for practitioners
and policy-makers. As Ball (1998: 77) has put it 'the policy entrepre-
neurs interests in terms of identity and career, are bound up directly

and immediately … with the success of their dissemination'. Taken to extremes, there are examples of school management academics not just providing research support for, but actually taking up key policy roles implementing OSI and OSL.[3] On the other hand education management perspectives which cannot be easily turned to the cause of post-welfarist school reform are less likely to find favour with policy-makers. Research contracts, consultancies and invitations to speak are all likely to be less forthcoming for textual dissenters and so it will be harder for them to construct the individual fabrications which are so much a part of 'getting ahead' as an academic in managerialist times. In contrast the policy sociologists who produce the kinds of critiques of post-welfarist school reform noted earlier and are most likely to be textual dissenters are typically under less pressure than school management and leadership academics to do 'useful' research and teaching. Indeed they can advance their careers through work which provides a trenchant critique of government policy.[4]

Conclusion

To the extent that they can be encouraged to genuinely incorporate more powerful critiques of post-welfarist school reform, academics working in higher education in the school leadership and management area could send out less apologetic messages and thus become a more potent force for good.

In the case of primarily problem-solving and overtly apologist analyses, the way forward is fairly clear. It is not hard to make the case that primarily problem-solving accounts should be rejected as being too socially and politically decontextualized and that academics should refuse to write at the level of 'tips' or in similarly reductive formats or accept the argument that busy practitioners need only

---

3. Michael Barber and David Hopkins, the previous and present heads of the DfES Standards and Effectiveness Units, have both formerly been professors of school improvement.
4. This is not to suggest there are no ethical tensions in the work of policy sociologists. Ball (1997: 258) argues that 'critical researchers, apparently safely ensconced in the moral high ground, nonetheless make a livelihood trading in the artefacts of misery and broken dreams of practitioners. None of us remains untainted by the incentives and disciplines of the new moral economy.'

problem-solving texts. (There being no point in writing 'simply' if to do so is to present practitioners with an analysis which is fundamentally inadequate.) Overt apologism can also be relatively easily challenged on the grounds that there is really no intellectually sound way that managerial reform can be accurately or ethically presented so unproblematically. Indeed both of these kinds of accounts are unacceptable enough within mainstream school management and leadership that challenging them could be regarded as a relatively uncontentious activity concerned with ensuring research and scholarly quality. As Goldstein and Woodhouse (2000: 357–358) have put it 'All research fields contain work demonstrating a wide range of "quality". One measure of the health of a field of study is the extent to which it progresses by eliminating the poor quality work, through a shared recognition of what counts as "good".'

By comparison, subtle apologism is much more difficult to counter since the authors of the texts so-characterized are likely to maintain that their work is critical enough. Building links to the theoretical or empirical arguments of textual dissenters may be one way of encouraging such authors to incorporate more powerful social and political critiques. But it also has to be recognized that strong critical arguments will often not be picked up because attention to the limitations of post-welfarist school reform undoubtedly has its costs for academics working in higher education in the area of school management and leadership. The subtle apologists in this area may indeed be at least partly blind to the ideologically and epistemologically situated nature of their intellectual position as Fielding (1997) suggests. But it is also likely that they provide a good example of the (uneasy) ethical accommodation needed of academics working in relatively applied areas of higher education if they are to acknowledge the problems created in their subject area by managerialism and yet want to prosper in their academic field in managerialist times.

Bibliography

Abbs, P. (1997) 'The ethical and the aesthetic in higher education', *Reflection on Higher Education*, Vol. 9, pp. 22–24.

Advisory Group on Citizenship (Crick 1) (1998) *Education for Citizenship and the Teaching for Democracy in Schools*, London: QCA, available at www.dfes.gov.uk/citizenship.

Advisory Group on Citizenship (Crick 2) (2000) *Citizenship for 16–19 Year Olds in Education and Training*, Further Education Funding Council. www.dfes.gov.uk/citizenship.

Advisory Group on Citizenship ('Crick Report') (1998) *Education for Citizenship and the Teaching of Democracy in Schools*, London: QCA.

Ahier, John, John Beck and Rob Moore (2003) *Graduate Citizens? Issues of Citizenship and Higher Education*, London: RoutledgeFalmer.

Alexiadou, N. (2002) 'Social inclusion and social exclusion in England: tensions in education policy', *Journal of Education Policy*, 17, 1, pp. 71–86.

Ambrey, Susan (2004) 'Rekindling meaning in undergraduate education: institutional culture and character development', *Journal of College and Character*, 2.

Anderson, J. (1980) 'Education and practicality', in *Education and Inquiry*, Oxford: Basil Blackwell, pp. 153–158.

Anne Frank (2001) Directed by Robert Dornheim. Performed by Ben Kingsley, Brenda Blethyn, and Hannah Taylor Gordon. Touchstone Films.

Annette, John (1999) 'Citizenship studies, service learning and higher education', in Roy Gardner *et al.*, eds, *Education for Values*, London: Kogan Page (reissued in paperback in 2003).

Annette, John (2000) 'Education for citizenship, civic participation and experiential and service learning in the community', in D. Lawton, J. Cairns and R. Gardner, eds, *Education for Democratic Citizenship*, London: Continuum.

Annette, John (2003a) '"International service learning," Frontiers', *Journal of International Education*.

Annette, John (2003b) 'Community, politics and citizenship education', in Andrew Lockyer, Bernard Crick and John Annette, eds, *Education for Democratic Citizenship*, Aldershot: Ashgate.

Annette, John, Susan Buckingham-Hatfield and Elaine Slater-Simmons, eds (2000) *Student – Community Partnerships in Higher Education*, London: CSV Publications.

Archbishop of Canterbury's Commission on Urban Priority Areas (1985) *Faith in the City*, London: Church House Publishing.

Archer, L. and H. Yamashita (2003) '"Knowing, their limits"? Identities, inequalities and inner city school leavers' post 16 aspirations', *Journal of Education Policy*, 18, 1, pp. 53–69.

Aristotle (1941) 'The history of animals', in R. McKeon, ed., *The Basic Works of Aristotle*, New York: Random House, pp. 633–642.

Aristotle (1980) *Nicomachean Ethics* (D. Ross, Trans.), New York: Oxford University Press.

Aristotle (1992) *The Politics* (T. A. Sinclair, Trans.) Harmondsworth: Penguin.

Arjen, E. J. and B. Jickling (2003) '"Sustainability" in higher education: from doublethink and newspeak to critical thinking and meaningful learning', *Higher Education Policy*, 15, 2, pp. 121–131.

Arnold, M. (1864/2003) 'The function of criticism at the present time', in S. Collini, ed., *Culture and Anarchy and Other Writings*, Cambridge: Cambridge University Press, pp. 26–51.

Arthur, J. (2000) *Schools and Community: The Communitarian Agenda in Education*, London: Falmer Press.

Arthur, J. (2002) *Education with Character: The Moral Economy of Schooling*, London: Routledge.

Astin, Alexander (2002) 'Higher education and the cultivation of citizenship', in Dwight Allman and Michael Beaty, eds, *Cultivating Citizens*, Lexington Books.

Ball, S. J. (1994) *Educational Reform: A Critical and Post-Structural Approach*, Buckingham Open University Press.

Ball, S. J. (1997) 'Policy sociology and critical social research: a personal review of recent education policy and policy research', *British Educational Research Journal*, 23, 3, pp. 257–274.

Ball, S. J. (1998) 'Educational studies, policy entrepreneurship and social theory', in R. Slee, S. Tomlinson with G. Weiner, eds, *School Effectiveness from Whom?*, London and Bristol, PA: Falmer.

Barber, Benjamin (1992) *An Aristocracy of Everyone*, Oxford: Oxford University Press.

Barber, Benjamin (1998a) *A Passion for Democracy*, Princeton University Press.

Barber, Benjamin (1998b) *A Place for Us: How to Make Society Civil and Democracy Strong*, New York: Hill and Wang.

Barnett, J. (1974) 'The influence of community', in K. G. Collier, P. Tomlinson and J. Wilson, eds, *Values and Moral Development in Higher Education*, London: Croom Helm.

Barnett, R. (1990) *The Idea of Higher Education*, Milton Keynes: Open University Press.

Barnett, R. (2000) *Realizing the University in an Age of Supercomplexity*, Buckingham: SRHE/Open University Press.

Barnett, R. (2003) *Beyond All Reason: Living with Ideology in the University*, Buckingham: SRHE/Open University Press.

Barnett, Ronald, ed. (1994) *Academic Community: Discourse or Discord?*, London: Jessica Kingsley Publications.

Barnett, Ronald and Paul Standish (2003) 'Higher education and the university in Blake', in N. Smeyers, P. Smith and P. Standish, eds, *The Blackwell Guide to the Philosophy of Education*, Oxford: Blackwell Publishing.

Battistoni, Richard (2002) *Civic Engagement Across the Curriculum*, London: Campus Compact.

Battistoni, Richard and William Hudson, eds (1997) *Experiencing Citizenship: Concepts and Models for Service Learning in Political Science*, Washington DC: American Association for Higher Education.

Bauman, Zygmunt (2000) *Community*, Cambridge: Polity Press.

Beck, J. (1998) *Morality and Citizenship in Education*, London: Cassell.

Beecher, Tony (2003) *Academic Tribes and Territories (SRHE)*, London: Open University Press, revised edition.

Bellah, Robert *et al.* (1996) *Habits of the Heart*, 2nd edn, Berkeley: University of California Press.

Bender, Thomas and Carl Schorske, eds (1997) *American Academic Culture in Transition*, Princeton University Press.

Benson, Lee and Ira Harkavy (2002) 'Democratization over commodification! An action orientated strategy to overcome the contradictory legacy of American higher education', *The Journal of Public Affairs*, VI (Supplemental Issue 1: Civic Engagement and Higher Education).

Blackmore, J. (1999) *Troubling Women, Feminism, Leadership and Educational Change*, Buckingham and Philadelphia: Open University Press.

Blake, N., R. Smith and P. Standish (1998) *The Universities We Need: Higher Education After Dearing*, London: Kogan Page.

Bloom, A. (1987) *The Closing of the American Mind*, Harmondsworth: Penguin Books.

Bloom, A. (1998) *The Closing of the American Mind*, New York: Simon and Schuster.

Blunkett, David (2001) *Politics and Progress: Renewing Democracy and Civil Society*, London: Politico's Publishing.

Bok, Derek (2004) 'Universities and the decline of civic responsibility', *Journal of College and Character*, 2.

Boss, J. A. (1996) 'The effect of community service work on the moral development of college ethics students', *Journal of Moral Education*, 23, pp. 183–198.

Boucher, David and Andrew Vincent, eds (2000) *British Idealism and Political Theory*, Edinburgh University Press.

Bouyer, L. (1958) *Newman*, London: Burns and Oates.

Bowe, R., S. Ball and A. Gold (1992) *Reforming Education and Changing Schools: Case Studies in Policy Sociology*, London: Routledge.

Boyer, Ernest (1987) *Carnegie Commission Report on the Undergraduate Experience in America*, Washington DC.

Boyte, Harry and Nancy Kari (2000) 'Renewing the democratic spirit in American colleges and universities: higher education as public work', in Ehrlich, ed. *Civic Responsibility of Higher Education*, American Council on Education: Oryx Press.

Bramley, W. (1977) *Personal Tutoring in Higher Education*, University of Guildford: Society for Research into Higher Education.

Brennan, John and Brenda Little (1996) *A Review of Work Based Learning in Higher Education*, London: DfEE.

Bridges, D. (2003) '"Fiction written under oath"? ethics and epistemology in educational research' Paper presented to the Philosophy of Education Society of Great Britain SE Branch, Canterbury Christ Church University College, Canterbury, Kent, UK, 7 October.

Brooks, David (2001) 'The organization kid', *The Atlantic Monthly*, April, pp. 40–54.

Brooks, David (2002) 'Making it: Love and success at America's finest universities', *The Weekly Standard*, 23 December, Vol. 008, Issue 15.

Brothers, J. (1971) *Residence and Student Life: A Sociological Inquiry into Residence in Higher Education*, London: Tavistock Press.

Bush, T. (2003) *Theories of Educational Management*, 2nd edn, London: Paul Chapman.

Callan, Eamon (1997) *Creating Citizens: Political Education and Liberal Democracy*, Oxford: Oxford University Press.

Camic, C. (1983) *Experience and Enlightenment*, Chicago: Chicago University Press.

Campbell, David (2000) 'Social capital and service learning', PS: *Political Science and Politics*, 33, 4.

Canning, R. (2003) 'Curriculum discourses in post-compulsory education: a project on the introduction of "higher still" in Scotland', *Journal of Education Policy*, 18, 4, pp. 439–451.

Carey, George and Bruce Frohnen, eds (1998) *Community and Tradition*, New York: Rowman and Littlefield.

Carr, D. and J. Steutel, eds (1999) 'Pointers, problems and prospects', *Virtue Ethics and Moral Education*, London and New York: Routledge, pp. 241–255.

Carr, E. II. (1975) *What is History?*, Harmondsworth: Penguin.

Carter, C. (1980) *Higher Education for the Future*, Oxford: Blackwell.

Clare, J. (2003) 'Graduates are left with a £9,000 hangover', *The Daily Telegraph*, Wednesday 19 November, p. 3.

Coare, Pam and Rennie Johnston, eds (2003) *Adult Learning, Citizenship and Community Voices*, London: NIACE.

Coffield, Frank and Bill Williamson (1997) *Repositioning Higher Education*, Buckingham: SRHE/Open University Press.

Colby, A. (2002) 'Whose values anyway?' *Journal of College and Character*, 2.

Colby, Anne, Thomas Ehrlich, Elizabeth Beaumont and Jason Stephens (2003). *Educating Citizens: Preparing America's Undergraduates for Lives of Moral and Civic Responsibility*. San Francisco: Jossey-Bass.

Collier, G. (1993) 'Learning moral judgement in higher education', *Studies in Higher Education*, 18, 3, pp. 287–297.

Collier, G. (1997) 'Learning moral commitment in higher education', *Journal of Moral Education*, 26, 1, pp. 73–85.

Collier, K. G., P. Tomlinson and J. Wilson, eds (1974) *Values and Moral Development in Higher Education*, London: Croom Helm.

Collini, Stefan (2003) 'HiEdBiz', in *The London Review of Books*, 6 November, Vol. 25, p. 21.

Cotterill, P. and R. L. Waterhouse (1996) 'The demise of the personal tutorial in higher education', in D. Jary and M. Parker, eds, *The New Higher Education*, Stoke-on-Trent: Staffordshire University Press.

Council of Europe (2000a) Joint Meeting of Working Party and Contact Group on Universities as Sites of Citizenship. Compendium American Universities. Strasbourg, Council of Europe.

Council of Europe (2000b) Joint Meeting of Working Party and Contact Group on Universities as Sites of Citizenship. Compendium (provisional version) European Universities. Strasbourg, Council of Europe.

Cowan, J. (1998) *On Becoming an Innovative University Teacher: Refection in Action*. Buckingham: SRHE and Open University Press.

Crick, Bernard (2000a) *In Defence of Politics*, 5th edn, London: Continuum.

Crick, Bernard (2000b) *Essays on Citizenship*, London: Continuum.

Crick, Bernard, ed. (2001) *Citizens: Towards a Citizenship Culture*, Oxford: Blackwell Publishers.

Crick, Bernard (2002) *Democracy*, Oxford: Oxford University Press.

Cruz, Nadine and Dwight Giles, Jr (2000) 'Where's the community in service-learning Research?', *Michigan Journal of Community Service Learning*, Special Issue Fall, 2000 CVCP, Universities and Community, CVCP.

Dagger, Richard (1997) *Civic Virtues: Rights, Citizenship and Republican Liberalism*, Oxford: Oxford University Press.

Davie, G. (1961) *The Democratic Intellect in Scotland and her Universities in the Nineteenth Century*, Edinburgh: Edinburgh University Press.

Davies, B. and L. Ellison (1997) *School Leadership for the 21st Century*, London: Routledge.

Davies, Ian *et al.* (1999) *Good Citizenship and Educational Provision*, London: Falmer Press.

DEA (Development Education association) (2002) *Globalisation and Higher Education: Guidance on Ethical Issues Arising from International Academic Activities.* London: DEA.

De Groof, Jan and Paul Mahieu (1993) *De school komt tot haar recht*, Leuven (Belgum): Garant.

Delanty, Gerard (2000) *Citizenship in a Global Age: Society, Culture, Politics*, Buckingham: Open University Press.

Delanty, Gerard (2001) *Challenging Knowledge: The University in the Knowledge Society*, Buckingham: The Society for Research into Higher Education and Open University Press.

Delanty, Gerard (2003) *Community*, London: Routledge.

Dempster, N. and L. Logan (1998) 'Expectations of school leaders: an Australian study', in J. MacBeath, ed., *Effective School Leadership: Responding to Change*, London: Paul Chapman.

Dempster, N. and P. Mahony (1998) 'Ethical challenges in school leadership', in J. MacBeath, ed., *Effective School Leadership: Responding to Change*, London: Paul Chapman.

DETR (1998) *Modern Local Government: In Touch With the People*, London: HMSO.

Devine, Richard, Joseph Favazza and Michael McLain, eds (2002) *From Cloister to Commons: Concepts and Models for Service Learning in Religious Studies*, Washington DC: American Association of Higher Education.

Dijkstra, Anne Bert, Japp Dronkers and Roelande Hofman, eds (1997) *Verzuiling in het onderwijs*, Groningen: Wolters-Noordhoff.

Dill, D. D. (20 03) 'Allowing the market to rule: the case of the United States', *Higher Education Quarterly*, 57, 2, pp. 136–157.

Dionne, E. J., Jr., ed. (1998) *Community Works: The Revival of Civil Society in America*, Washington DC: Brookings Institute Press.

Dionne, E. J., Jr. *et al.*, eds (2003) *United We Serve: National Service and the Future of Citizenship*, Washington DC: Brookings Institute Press.

Dower, Nigel (2003) *An Introduction to Global Citizenship*, Edinburgh: Edinburgh University Press.

Drew, Sue (1998) *Key Skills in Higher Education: Background and Rationale*, London: SEDA.

Duff, A. S. (2003) 'Higher education teaching: a communication perspective', *Active Learning in Higher Education*, 4, 3, pp. 256–270.

Dyer, C. (2003) 'New Britons to pledge loyalty to country: how they do it in Canada', *The Guardian*, 7, 26 July.

Edwards, Bob, Michael Foley and Mario Diani (2001) *Beyond Tocqueville: Civil society and the Social Capital Debate in Comparative Perspective*, Hanover: Tufts University Press.

Eesley, Chuck (2002) 'Figuring Out Life's Most Important Values', available at: www.collegevalues.org/reflections.cfm?id = 676&a = 1.

Ehrlich, Thomas, ed. (2000) *Civic Responsibility of Higher Education*, American Council on Education: Oryx Press.

Ehrlich, Thomas, Anne Colby *et al.* (2003) *Education Citizens*, San Francisco: Jossey-Bass.

Eljamal, M. B., J. S. Stark, G. L. Arnold and S. Sharp (1999) 'Intellectual development: a complex teaching goal', *Studies in Higher Education*, Vol. 24, pp. 7–25.

Elliott, Jane *et al.* (1996) *Communities and Their Universities*, London: Lawrence and Wishart.

Englund, Tomas (2002) 'Higher education, democracy and citizenship – the democratic potential of the University?', *Studies in Philosophy and Education*, 21, 4–5, pp. 281–287.

Enos, Sandra and Keith Morton (2002) 'Building deeper civic relationships and new and improved citizens', *Journal of Public Affairs*, VI (Supplemental issue: Civic Engagement and Higher Education).

Erickson, Joseph and Jeffrey Anderson, eds (1997) *Learning with the Community: Concepts and Models for Service Learning in Teacher Education*, Washington DC: American Association for Higher Education.

Etzioni, Amitai (1995) *The Spirit of Community*, London: Fontana Press.

Evans, M. (2004) 'Academicus superciliosus: the beast revisited', in D. Hayes, ed., *The RoutledgeFalmer Guide to Key Debates in Education*, London: RoutledgeFalmer.

Eyler, Janet and Dwight Giles, Jr. (1999) *Where's the Learning in Service Leaning?*, San Francisco: Jossey-Bass.

Farnell, Richard (2001) 'Faith-communities, regeneration and social exclusion', *Community Development Journal*, 36, 4.

Farnell, Richard *et al.* (2003) '"Faith" in urban regeneration?', JRF/The Policy Press.

Faulks, Keith (2000) *Citizenship*, London: Routledge.

Faust, C. H. and J. Feingold (1969) *Approaches to Education for Character: Strategies for Change in Higher Education*, Conference on Science, Philosophy and Religion, Columbia: Columbia University Press.

Fielding, M. (1997) 'Beyond school effectiveness and school improvement: lighting the slow fuse of possibility', In J. White and M. Baber, eds, *Perspectives on School Effectiveness and School Improvement*, London: Institute of Education, pp. 137–160.

Fitz, J. (1999) 'Reflections on the field of educational managements studies', *Educational Management and Administration*, 27, 3, pp. 313–321.

Forsyth, A. and A. Furlong (2003) 'Access to higher education and disadvantaged young people', *British Educational Research Journal*, 28, 1, pp. 5–19.

Fowler, Robert Booth (1991) *The Dance With Community*, Lawrence: University of Kansas Press.

Frankfurt, Harry (1988) *The Importance of What We Care About*, New York: Cambridge University Press.

Frankl, V. E. (1984) *Man's Search for Meaning*, 3rd edn, New York: Simon and Schuster.

Frazer, Elizabeth (1999a) 'Introduction: the idea of political education', in *Oxford Review of Education*, 25, 1–2, pp. 5–22.

Frazer, Elizabeth (1999b) *The Problems of Communitarian Politics*, Oxford: Oxford University Press.

Frohnen, Bruce (1996) *The New Communitarians and the Crisis of Modern Liberalism*, Lawrence: The University of Kansas Press.

Fuller, Timothy ed. (1989) *The Voice of Liberal Learning: Michael Oakeshott on Education*, New Haven and London: Yale University Press.

Furedi, F. (2003) *Therapy Culture: Cultivating Vulnerability in an Uncertain Age*, London and New York: Routledge.

Further Education Funding Council, Citizenship for 16–19 Year Olds in Education and Training (2000) Report of the Advisory Group to the Secretary of State for Education and Employment, FEFC, available at www.dfes.gov.uk/citizenship.

Gayle, V., D. Berridge and R. Davies (2002) 'Young people's entry into higher education: quantifying influential factors', *Oxford Review of Education*, 28, 1, pp. 5–20.

Gellert, C. (1981) *A Comparative Study of the Changing Functions of English and German Universities*, unpublished PhD thesis, University of Cambridge.

Gelmon, Sherrill *et al.* (2001) *Assessing Service-Learning and Civic Engagement*, Campus Compact.

Gewirtz, S. (2002) *The Managerial School*, London: Routledge.

Gillborn, D. and D. Youdell (2000) *Rationing Education Policy, Reform and Equity*, Buckingham: Open University Press.

Glaser, B. and A. Strauss (1967) *The Discovery of Grounded Theory*, Chicago, IL: Aldine.

Gleeson, D. and C. Husbands, eds (2001) *The Performing School*, London: RoutledgeFalmer.

Glenn, Charles L. (2000) *The Ambiguous Embrace: Government and Faith-based Schools and Social Agencies*, Princeton: Princeton University Press.

Goldstein, H. and G. Woodhouse (2000) 'School effectiveness research and educational policy', *Oxford Review of Education*, 26, 3 and 4, pp. 353–363.

Goodlad, S. (1976) *Conflict and Consensus in Higher Education*, London: Hodder and Stoughton.

Goodlad, S. (1999) 'Benchmarks and templates – some notes and queries from a sceptic', in H. Smith, M. Armstrong and S. Brown, eds, *Benchmarking and Threshold Standards in Higher Education*, London: Kogan Page.

Gordon, Peter and John White (1972) *Philosophers as Educational Reformers: The Influence of Idealism on British Educational Thought and Practice*, London: Routledge.

Gorham, Eric (1992) *National Service, Citizenship and Political Education*, New York: SUNY Press.

Grace, G. (1995) *School Leadership: Beyond Educational Management*, London and Washington DC: Falmer.

Grace, G. (2000) 'Research and the challenges of contemporary school leadership: the contribution of critical scholarship', *British Journal of Educational Studies*, 48, 3, pp. 231–247.

Grace, G. (2003) 'British forward' to Arthur, J. (2003) *Education with Character: The Moral Economy of Schooling*, London and New York: RoutledgeFalmer, pp. x–xi.

Graham, Gordon (2002) *Universities: The Recovery of an Idea*, Thorverton: Imprint Academic.

Gray, J. (2001) 'Introduction: building for improvement and sustaining change in schools serving disadvantaged communities', in M. Maden, ed., *Success Against the Odds – Five Years On*, London: RoutledgeFalmer.

Gronn, P. (2003) *The New World of Educational Leaders*, London: Paul Chapman.

Guarasci, Richard and Grant Cornwall, eds (1997) *Democratic Education in an Age of Difference*, San Francisco: Jossey-Bass.

Gunter, H. (2001) *Leaders and Leadership in Education*, London: Paul Chapman.

Hall, Peter (2002) 'The role of Government and the distribution of social capital', in Robert D. Putnam, ed., *Democracies in Flux*, Oxford: Oxford University Press.

Hall, I. and D. Hall (2002) 'Incorporating change through reflection: community based learning', in R. Macdonald and J. Wisdom, eds, *Academic and Educational Development: Research, Evaluation and Changing Practice in Higher Education*, London: Kogan Page.

Halsey, A. H. (1995) *The Decline of Donnish Dominion*, rev. edn, Oxford: Clarendon Press.

Hargreaves, David (1997) *The Mosaic of Learning*, London: Demos.

Harkavy, Ira and Lee Benson (1998) 'De-platonising and democratizing education as the bases of service learning', in Robert Rhoads, ed., *Academic Service-Learning: A Pedagogy of Action and Reflection*, San Francisco: Jossey-Bass.

Harvey, Lee *et al*. (1998) *Work Experience: Expanding Opportunities for Under-graduates*, Centre for Research into Quality.

Haselgrove, S., ed. (1994) *The Student Experience*, Buckingham: Open University Press.

Hatch, S. (1974) 'Institutional contexts', in K. G. Collier, P. Tomlinson and J. Wilson, eds, *Values and Moral Development in Higher Education*, London: Croom Helm.

Hatcher, R. (1998) 'Labour, official school improvement and equality', *Journal of Education Policy*, 13, 4, pp. 485–499.

Hayes, D. (2004a) 'The role of the teacher', in D. Cummings, ed., Ideas Intellectuals and the Public, *Critical Review of International Social and Political Philosophy*, Special Edition 2004: forthcoming.

Hayes, D. (2004b) *Defending Higher Education: The Crisis of Confidence in the Academy*, London and New York: RoutledgeFalmer.

Heffner, Gail Gunst and Claudia Devries Beversluis, eds (2003) *Commitment and Connection: Service Learning and Christian Higher Education*, New York: Rowman and Littlefield.

Henry, C. (1994) 'An ethical perspective', in S. Haselgrove, ed., *The Student Experience*, Buckingham: Open University Press.

Hesser, Gary (2003) 'Review essay: faith-based service learning: back to the future', *Michigan Journal of Community Service Learning*, 10, 1, Fall.

Higher Education Foundation (1997) *Reflection on Higher Education*, Vol. 9.

Hill, Paul T. and Mary Beth Celio (1998) *Fixing Urban Schools*, Washington DC: Brookings Institution Press.

Hinton, P. (1947) *The University of Birmingham*, Birmingham: Cornish Brothers.

Hoggett, Paul, ed. (1997) *Contested Communities*, Bristol: The Policy Press.

Holroyd, C. (2000) 'Are assessors professional? student assessment and the professionalisation of academics', *Active Learning in Higher Education*, 1, 1, pp. 28–44.

Horne, H. and S. Brown (1997) *500 Tips for School Improvement*, London: Kogan Page.

Ingrams, R. (1995) *Muggeridge: The Biography*, San Francisco: Harper.

Jacoby, Barbara, ed. (1996) *Service Learning in Higher Education*, San Francisco: Jossey-Bass.

Jacoby, Barbara (2003) *Building Partnerships for Service Learning*, San Francisco: Jossey-Bass.

Jenkins, K. (1991) *Re-Thinking History*, London: Routledge.

Jongbloed, B. (2003) 'Marketisation in higher education, Clark's Triangle and the essential ingredients of markets', *Higher Education Quarterly*, 57, 2, pp. 110–135.

Jorgenson, Brian (2000) 'Nowhere motel, light beyond being', *Journal of Education*. This chapter builds on ideas explored in an article I wrote for the special issue of the Journal of Education, 'Can virtue be taught at the university?' *Journal of Education*, 182, 2, p. 57.

Kahne, Joseph *et al.* (2000) 'Service-learning and citizenship: directions for research', *Michigan Journal of Community Service Learning*.

Kearn, Thomas (2000) 'Remarks at the 10th Annual Institute on College Student Values', 3–5 February Tallahassee, Florida, available at: http://www.collegevalues.org/articles.cfm?a=1&id=44.

Ker, I. (1989) *The Genius of John Henry Newman*, Oxford: Clarendon Press.

Kerckhoff, A. C., K. Fogelman and J. Manlove (1997) 'Staying ahead: the middle classes and school reform in England and Wales', *Sociology of Education*, 70, 1, pp. 19–35.

Kerr, David (1997) *Citizenship Education Revisited-National Case Study-England*, Slough: National Foundation for Educational Research (NFER) (rev. edn, 1999).

Kimball, Bruce A. (1995) *Orators and Philosophers: A History of the Idea of Liberal Education*, The College Board, Rev. edn.

Kolb, David (1998) *Experiential Learning*, Englewood Cliffs, NJ: Prentice Hall.

Kors, Alan Charles and Harvey A. Silverglate (1998) *The Shadow University: The Betrayal of Liberty in America's Campuses*, New york: The Free Press.

Krauth, Kevin (2002) 'Sharpening the competitive edge: when competition becomes dangerous', available at: http://www.collegevalues.org/reflections.cfm?id=715&a=1.

Kruchov, C., J. MacBeath and K. Riley (1998) 'Introduction', in J. MacBeath, ed., *Effective School Leadership: Responding to Change*, London: Paul Chapman.

Lawless, P. *et al.* (1998) 'Community based initiative and state urban policy: the Church Urban Fund', *Regional Studies*, 32, 2.

Leicester, M., C. Modgil and S. Modgil, eds (2000) *Education, Culture and Values. Volume VI: Politics, Education and Citizenship*, London: Falmer.

Lemon, M. C. (1995) *The Discipline of History and the History of Thought*, London: Routledge.

Lerner, Michael (1997) *The Politics of Meaning*, New york: Addison and Wesley.

Lisman, C. David (1998) *Toward a Civil Society: Civic Literacy and Service Learning*, London: Bergin and Garvey.

Lister, Ruth (2003) *Citizenship: Feminist Perspectives*, 2nd edn, London: Palgrave.

Little, Adrian (2002) *The Politics of Community*, Edinburgh: Edinburgh University Press.

Little, Brenda (1998) *Developing Key Skills Through Work Placement*, London: CIHE.

Lockyer, Andrew, Bernard Crick and John Annette, eds (2003) *Education for Democratic Citizenship: Issues of Theory and Practice*, Aldershot: Ashgate.

Losin, P. (1998) 'Education and Plato's parable of the cave', Journal of Education, 178, 3, pp. 49–66.

Lowndes, Victoria *et al.* (1998) *Enhancing Public Participation in Local Government: Research Report*, London: DETR.

Lukka, Pryia and Michael Locke with Andri Soteri-Procter (2003) *Faith and Voluntary Action: Community, Values and Resources*, Institute for Volunteering Research.

MacBeath, J., ed. (1998a) *Effective School Leadership: Responding to Change*, London: Paul Chapman.

MacBeath, J. (1998b) 'Seven selected heresies of leadership', in J. MacBeath, ed., *Effective School Leadership: Responding to Change*, London: Paul Chapman.

Macfarlane, B. (2004) *Teaching with Integrity: The Ethics of Higher Education Practice*, London and New York: RoutledgeFalmer.

MacIntyre, A. (1984) *After Virtue: A Study in Moral Theory*, Notre Dame: University of Notre Dame Press.

MacIntyre, A. (2001) 'Catholic universities: dangers, hopes, choices', in R. E. Sullivan, ed., *Higher Learning and Catholic Traditions*, Notre Dame IN: Notre Dame Press.

Marquand, David (1997) *The New Reckoning*, Cambridge: Polity Press.

Marsden, George M. (1994) *The Soul of the American University: From Protestant Establishment to Established Nonbelief*, New York: Oxford University Press.

Marshall, T. H. (1950) *Citizenship and Social Class*, Cambridge: Cambridge University Press.

Maskell, D. and I. Robinson (2002) *The New Idea of a University*, Thorverton: Imprint Academic.

Mason, Andrew (2000) *Community, Solidarity and Belonging*, Cambridge: Cambridge University Press.

Matthews, Anne (1997) *Bright College Years: Inside the American Campus Today*, New York: Simon and Schuster.

Maynor, John (2003) *Republicanism in the Modern World*, Cambridge: Polity Press.

McCormick, James (1994) *Citizen's Service*, London: IPPR.

McIntyre, A. (1982) *After Virtue*, London: Duckworth.

McLaughlin, Terence H. (2000a) 'Citizenship education in England: the Crick report and beyond', *Journal of Philosophy of Education*, 34, 4.

McLaughlin, Terence H. (2000b) 'The European dimension of higher education: neglected claims and concepts', in F. Crawley, P. Smeyers, and P. Standish, eds, *Universities Remembering Europe: Nations, Culture and Higher Education*, New York and Oxford: Berghahn Books.

Miller, David (2000) 'Citizenship: what does it mean and why is it important?', in N. Pearce and J. Hallgarten, eds, *Tomorrow's Citizens: Critical Debates in Citizenship and Education*, London: IPPR.

Miller, David (2001) *Citizenship and National Identity*, Cambridge: Polity Press.

Moberly, W. (1949) *The Crisis of the University*, London: SCM.

Mohan, John (1994) 'What can you do for your country? arguments for and against Clinton's National Service Legislation', *Policy and Politics*, 22, 4.

Mohan, John (1997) 'Reconnecting the academy? community involvement in American and British Universities', in J. Elliott *et al.*, eds, *Communities and Their Universities*, London: Lawrence and Wishart.

Monsma, Stephen V. (1996) *When Sacred and Secular Mix*, Lanham (MD): Rowman and Littlefield.

Morgan, S. L. (1996) 'Trends in black-white differences in educational expectations 1980–1992', *Sociology of Education*, 69, 4, pp. 308–319.

Moskos, Charles (1998) *A Call to Service*, London: Free Press.

Mulhall, S. and A. Swift (1996) *Liberalism and Communitarianism*, 2nd edn, Oxford: Blackwells.

Nash, Victoria (2002) *Reclaiming Community*, London: IPPR.

National Committee of Inquiry into Higher Education (1997) (The Dearing Report) London: Department for Education and Employment.

National Committee of Inquiry into Higher Education-NICHE (1997) (The Dearing Report), *Higher Education in the Learning Society*.

Newman, J. H. (1852/1996) *The Idea of a University* (ed. F. M. Turner), New Haven and London: Yale University Press.

Newman, J. H. (1975) *The Idea of a University* (ed. I. T. Ker), Oxford: Oxford University Press.

Niblett, W. R. (1990) 'An absence of outrage: cultural change and values in british higher education 1930–1990', *Reflections on Higher Education*, 2, 2.

Nisbet, Robert A. (1971) *The Degradation of the Academic Dogma: The University in America, 1945–1970*, New York: Basic Books.

Northcott, Michael (1998) *Urban Theology: A Reader*, London: Cassell.

Nussbaum, Martha C. (1997) 'Cultivating Humanity', *A Classical Defense of Reform in Liberal Education*, Cambridge, MA: Harvard University Press.

Nussbaum, Martha C. (2002) 'Education for citizenship in an era of global connection', *Studies in Philosophy and Education*, 21, 4–5, pp. 289–303.

Oakeshott, M. (1962) *Rationalism in Politics and Other Essays*, London and New York: Methuen.

Oakeshott, M. (1972) 'Education: the engagement and its frustration', in R. F. Dearden, P. H. Hirst and R. S. Peters, eds, *Education and the Development of Reason*, London and Boston: Routledge and Kegan Paul, pp. 19–49.

Ofsted (office for standards in education) (2003) *National Curriculum Citizenship: Planning and Implementation 2002/3*, HMI 1606, London: Ofsted.

O'Hear, A. (1999) 'Enter the new robot Citizens', *Daily Mail*, 14 May.

Oldfield, Adrian (1990) *Citizenship and Community*, London: Routledge.

Orrill, Robert, ed. (1995) *The Condition of American Liberal Education*, The College Board.

Orrill, Robert, ed. (1998) *Education and Democracy: Re-imagining Liberal Learning in America*, The College Board.

Osler, Audrey (2000) 'The Crick report: difference, equality and racial justice', *The Curriculum Journal*, 11, 1, pp. 25–37.

Ozga, J. (2000) 'Leadership in education: the problem not the solution', *Discourses*, 21, 3, pp. 356–361.

Parlett, M. and D. Hamilton (1977) 'Evaluation as illumination', in D. Hamilton, D. Jenkins, C. King, B. MacDonald and M. Parlett, eds, *Beyond the Numbers Game*, London: Macmillan.

Parry, R. D. (1996) 'Morality and happiness: book IV of Plato's republic', *Journal of Education*, 178, 930, pp. 31–48.

Patterson, Lindsay (2003) 'The survival of the democratic intellect: academic values in Scotland and England', *Higher Education Quarterly*, 57, 1.

Pearce, N. and J. Hallgarten, eds (2000) *Tomorrow's Citizens: Critical Debates in Citizenship and Education*, London: Institute for Public Policy Research.

Pelikan, Jaroslav (1992) *The Idea of the University – A Reexamination*, New Haven and London: Yale University Press.

Perry, W. G. (1989) *Forms of Intellectual and Ethical Development in the College Years*, New York: Holt Rinehart and Winston.

Pettit, Philip (1997) *Republicanism: A Theory of Freedom and Government*, Oxford: Oxford University Press.

Plato (1989) *Symposium* (A. Nehamas and P. Woodrull, Trans.), Indianapolis: Hackett Publishing.

Plato (1992) *Republic* (G. M. A. Grube, Trans. C. D. C. Revere, Rev), Indianapolis: Hackett Publishing.

Potter, John (2002) *Active Citizenship in Schools*, London: Kogan Page.

Powell, Arthur G., Eleanor Farrar and David K. Cohen (1985) *The Shopping Mall High School*, Boston: Houghton Mifflin.

Pratchett, Lawrence, ed. (2000) *Renewing Local Democracy?*, London: Frank Cass.

Preston, John (2004) 'Lifelong learning and civic participation: inclusion, exclusion and community', in T. Schuller, J. Preston, C. Hammond, A. Brassett-Grundy and J. Bynner, eds, *The Benefits of Learning: The Impact of Education on Health, Family Life and Social Capital*, London: RoutledgeFalmer.

Pring, Richard (1999) 'Political education: relevance of the humanities', *Oxford Review of Education*, 25, 1/2, pp. 71–87.

Putnam, Robert D. (2000) *Bowling Alone in America*, New York: Simon and Schuster.

QAA (2001) *Medicine, Dentistry and Veterinary Medicine Draft Benchmark Statements*, Bristol: HEFCE.

Qualifications and Curriculum Authority, Education for Citizenship and the Teaching of Democracy in Schools (1998). Final Report of the Advisory Group on Citizenship, QCA, available at www.dfes.gov.uk/citizenship.

Reay, D., S. Ball and M. David (2002) ' "It's taking me a long time but I'll get there in the end"; mature students on access courses and higher education choice', *British Educational Research Journal*, 28, 1, pp. 5–19.

Reeher, Grant and Joseph Cammarano, eds (1997) *Education for Citizenship*, Lanham, MD: Rowman and Littlefield.

Reeves, M. (1988) *The Crisis in Higher Education*, Milton Keynes: Open University Press.

Reeves, J., L. Moos and J. Forrest (1998) 'The school leader's view', in J. MacBeath, ed., *Effective School Leadership: Responding to Change*, London: PCP.

Reisner, Edward H. (1992) *Nationalism and Education since 1789*, New York: Macmillan.

Reuben, Julie (1996) *The Making of the Modern University*, Chicago: The University of Chicago Press.

Rimmerman, Craig (1997) *The New Citizenship*, New York: Westview Press.

Rogow, F. (2001) 'The Merchants of Cool', Retrieved July 11, 2001, from PBS website: http://www.pbs.org/wgbh/pages/frontline/shows/cool/etc/synopsis.html.

Roochnik, D. (1997) 'Teaching virtue: the contrasting arguments (Dissoi Logoi) of Antiquity', *Journal of Education*, 179, 1, pp. 1–13.

Rothblatt, S. (1968) *The Revolution of the Dons*, London: Faber and Faber.

Rothblatt, S. (1976) *Tradition and Change in English Liberal Education*, London: Faber and Faber.

Rowland, S. (2000) *The Enquiring University Teacher*, Buckingham: SRHE/Open University Press.

Russell, B. (1940) *A History of Western Philosophy*, London: George Allen and Unwin Ltd.

Russell, Conrad (1993) *Academic Freedom*, London: Routledge.

Ryan, A. (1997) *John Dewey and the High Tide of American Liberalism*, London: W.W. Norton.

Ryan, A. (1999) *Liberal Anxieties and Liberal Education*, London: Profile Books.

Ryan, A. (2001) 'Perfection in politics and philosophy', in D. Palfreyman, ed., *The Oxford Tutorial*, Oxford: OxCHEPS, pp. 78–86.

Sacks, J. (2000) *The Politics of Hope*, London: Vintage.

Sacks, J. (2002) *The Dignity of Difference*, London: Continuum.

Samons, L. J., II. (2000) 'Socrates, virtue and the modern professor', *Journal of Education*, 182, 2, p. 23.

Sanford, N. (1969) 'The contribution of higher education to the life of society', in W. R. Niblett, ed., *Higher Education: Demands and Responses*, London: Tavistock Press.

Schneider, Barbara and David Stevenson (1999) *The Ambitious Generation: America's Teenagers, Motivated but Directionless*, New Haven: Yale University Press.

Schuller, T., J. Preston, C. Hammond, A. Brassett-Grundy and J. Bynner (2004) *The Benefits of Learning: The Impact of Education on Health, Family Life and Social Capital*, London: RoutledgeFalmer.

Scott, Peter (1995) *The Meanings of Higher Education (SRHE)*, London: Open University Press.

Sears, Alan (1996) ' "Something different to everyone": conceptions of citizenship and citizenship education', *Canadian and International Education*, 25, 2, pp. 1–16.

Sennett, R. (1998) *The Corrosion of Character*, New York: Norton.

Shaw, Peter (1979) 'Degenerate criticism', *Harper's 259*, October.

Shils, Edward (1997) *The Calling of Education: The Academic Ethic and Other Essays on Higher Education*, Chicago and London: University of Chicago Press.

Sirianni, Carmen and Lewis Friedland (2001) *Civic Innovation in America*, Berkely: University of California Press.

Soffer, Reba (1994) *Discipline and Power: The University, History and the Making of an English Elite, 1870–1930*, Stanford: Stanford University Press.

Stevens, Robert (2004) *University to UNI: The Politics of Higher Education in England since 1944*, London: Politico's.

Strand, Kerry, Sam Marullo, Nick Cutworth, Randy Stoecker and Patrick Donoghue (2003) *Community-Based Research and Higher Education*, San Francisco: Jossey-Bass.

Taylor, Marilyn (2003) *Public Policy in the Community*, London: Palgrave.

Telfer, E. (1980) *Happiness*, New York: St Martin's Press.

Thiessen, Elmer John (1993) *Teaching for Commitment*, Montreal: McGill-Queen's University Press.

Thompson, D. L. (1991) *Moral Values and Higher Education: A Nation at Risk*, New York: State University of New York Press.

Thrupp, M. and R. Wilmott (2003) *Educational Management in Managerialist Times: Beyond the Textual Apologists*, Buckingham: Open University Press.

Tigner, S. S. (1995) 'Signs of the soul', in G. S. Fain, ed., *Leisure and Ethics: Reflections on the Philosophy of Leisure*, Reston, VA: American Association for Leisure and Recreation, Vol. II, pp. 9–24.

Tomlinson, S. (2001) *Education in a Post-Welfare Society*, Buckingham and Philadelphia: Open University Press.

Tooley, J. (2000) *Reclaiming Education*, London: Cassell.

Torney-Purta, J., J. Schwille and J-A. Amadeo (1999) *Civic Education across Countries: Twenty-four National Case Studies from the IEA Civic Education Project*, Amsterdam: International Education Association.

Torrance, H. (2003) 'When is an "evaluation" not an evaluation? When it's sponsored by the QCA? A response to Lindsay and Lewis', *British Educational Research Journal*, 29, 2, pp. 169–175.

Travis, A. (2003) 'New Britons to pledge loyalty to country: Ministers want local flavour for Canadian-style citizenship ceremonies', *The Guardian*, 26 July, p. 7.

Universities, UK (2001) *The Regional Mission: The Regional Contribution of Higher Education – The National Report*, Universities, UK and HEFCE.

Vallely, P. (1998) *The New Politics*, London: SCM Press.

Verba, S., K. Schlozman and H. Brady (1995) *Voice and Equality: Civic Voluntarism in American Politics*, Cambridge: Harvard University Press.

Vulliamy, G. and R. Webb (2003) 'Bridging the cultural divide: the role of home-school support worker', *British Educational Research Journal*, 29, 3, pp. 285–305.

Wade, Rahima, ed. (1997) *Community Service-Learning*, New york: SUNY Press.

Wadell, Paul (1991) *Friendship and the Moral Life*, South Bend, IN: University of Notre Dame Press.

Wadell, Paul (2002) *Becoming Friends: Worship, Justice, and the Practice of Christian Friendship*, Grand Rapids, MI: Brazos Press.

Waldman, Steve (1995) *The Bill: How Legislation Really Becomes Law – the Case Study of the National Service Bill*, New York: Penguin Books.

Warnock, M. (1975) *Times Literary Supplement*, 18 April, p. 435.

Waterman, Alan (1997) *Service-Learning: Applications from the Research*, London: Lawrence Erlbaum Publishers.

Watson, David and Richard Taylor (1998) *Lifelong Learning and the University: A Post-Dearing Agenda*, London: Falmer Press.

Weber, Max (1946) 'Science as a vocation' (Wissenschaft als Beruf, 1919), in H. H. Gerth and C. Wright Mills, eds and trans., *From Max Weber: Essays in Sociology*, New York: Oxford University Press.

Weil, Susan Warner and Ian McGill, eds (1989) *Making Sense of Experiential Learning (SRHE)*, London: Open University Press.

White, J. (1997) 'Philosophy and the aims of higher education', *Studies in Higher Education*, 22, 1, pp. 7–17.

Wilmott, R. (1999) 'School effectiveness research: an ideological commitment?', *Journal of Philosophy of Education*, 33, 2, pp. 253–268.

Winch, Donald (1978) *Adam Smith's Politics*, Cambridge: Cambridge University Press.

Wolfe, Alan (2001) *Moral Freedom: The Impossible Idea That Defines the Way We Live Now*, New York: W.W. Norton and Company.

Wuthnow, Robert (1996) *Christianity and Civil Society: The Contemporary Debate*, Philadelphia: Trinity Press.

Wuthnow, Robert (1997) *Loose Connections*, Cambridge: Harvard University Press.

Yorke, M., P. Bridges and H. Woolf (2000) 'Mark distribution and marking policies in UK higher education: some challenging issues', *Active Learning in Higher Education*, 1, 1, pp. 7–27.

Youniss, J. and M. Yates (1997) *Community Service and Social Responsibility in Youth*, Chicago: University of Chicago Press.

Youniss, J., J. A. McClellan and M. Yates (1997) 'What we know about engendering civic identity', *American Behavioural Scientists*, 40, 5.

Zweig, F. (1963) *The Student in an Age of Anxiety: A Survey of Oxford and Manchester Students*, London: Heinemann.

Index